Lua Quick Start Guide

The easiest way to learn Lua programming

Gabor Szauer

BIRMINGHAM - MUMBAI

Lua Quick Start Guide

Copyright © 2018 Packt Publishing

Commissioning Editor: Richa Tripathi
Acquisition Editor: Noyonika Das
Content Development Editor: Roshan Kumar
Technical Editor: Sushmeeta Jena
Copy Editor: Safis Editing
Project Coordinator: Hardik Bhinde
Proofreader: Safis Editing
Indexer: Aishwarya Gangawane
Graphics: Jason Monteiro
Production Coordinator: Shantanu Zagade

First published: July 2018

Production reference: 1250718

Published by Packt Publishing Ltd.
Livery Place
35 Livery Street
Birmingham
B3 2PB, UK.

ISBN 978-1-78934-322-9

www.packtpub.com

`mapt.io`

Mapt is an online digital library that gives you full access to over 5,000 books and videos, as well as industry leading tools to help you plan your personal development and advance your career. For more information, please visit our website.

Why subscribe?

- Spend less time learning and more time coding with practical eBooks and Videos from over 4,000 industry professionals

- Improve your learning with Skill Plans built especially for you

- Get a free eBook or video every month

- Mapt is fully searchable

- Copy and paste, print, and bookmark content

PacktPub.com

Did you know that Packt offers eBook versions of every book published, with PDF and ePub files available? You can upgrade to the eBook version at `www.PacktPub.com` and as a print book customer, you are entitled to a discount on the eBook copy. Get in touch with us at `service@packtpub.com` for more details.

At `www.PacktPub.com`, you can also read a collection of free technical articles, sign up for a range of free newsletters, and receive exclusive discounts and offers on Packt books and eBooks.

Contributors

About the author

Gabor Szauer graduated from Full Sail University with a bachelor's degree in game development. He has been making video games professionally since 2010. He has worked on games for the Nintendo 3DS, Xbox 360, browser-based games, as well as games for iOS and Android. Gabor loves to teach, especially game development and programming. He has previously written the *Game Physics Cookbook* and is looking forward to producing much more content for those who want to learn.

> *"Give someone a program, you frustrate them for a day; teach them how to program, you frustrate them for a lifetime."*

- David Leinweber

About the reviewer

Jayant Varma is an author of books on iOS development (Swift, Objective-C, and Xcode); Bash & Lua was his first book. He has been the technical editor for several Packt books. An academician at JCU, he mentored students for the Apple Swift Course at RMIT. He was the IT manager for BMW & Nissan, and as a development manager for an ASX-listed company, he contracted and built several mobile apps for small-to-large organizations in Australia. He has conducted workshops and spoken at meetups and events. He started OZApps and provides consulting and development services.

Packt is searching for authors like you

If you're interested in becoming an author for Packt, please visit `authors.packtpub.com` and apply today. We have worked with thousands of developers and tech professionals, just like you, to help them share their insight with the global tech community. You can make a general application, apply for a specific hot topic that we are recruiting an author for, or submit your own idea.

Table of Contents

Preface

Lua is a small, powerful, and extendable programming language that can be used to learn to program, write games and applications, or as an embedded scripting language. This book is the easiest way to learn Lua; it introduces you to the basics of Lua and helps you understand the problems it solves.

You will work with the basic language features, the libraries Lua provides, and powerful topics such as object-oriented programming. Every aspect of programming in Lua—variables, data types, functions, tables, arrays and objects—is covered in sufficient detail for you to get started. You will also find out about Lua's module system and how to interface with the operating system.

After reading this book, you will be ready to use Lua as a programming language to write code that can interface with the operating system, automate tasks, make playable games, and much more. This book is a solid starting point for those who want to learn Lua and then move on to other technologies, such as Love2D, to make games.

Who this book is for

This book is for developers who want to get up and running with Lua. This book is ideal for programmers who want to learn to embed Lua in their own applications, and is also ideal for beginner programmers who have never coded before. Starting with an introduction to the Lua language, you will learn how to create variables and use loops and functions. You will learn advanced concepts, such as creating an object-oriented class system using only Lua tables. We look at the standard Lua libraries and learn how to debug Lua code. We will use Lua as an embedded scripting language and learn about the Lua C API in detail.

What this book covers

Chapter 1, *Introduction to Lua*, serves as an introduction to Lua by answering the question what is Lua? Next, the chapter walks the reader through downloading and installing the appropriate Lua binaries, as well as Visual Studio Code. Visual Studio Code is the code editor we will be using throughout this book to edit Lua files.

Chapter 2, *Working with Lua*, is a primer on the basics of the Lua language. For those who have not programmed before, this chapter teaches the basic concepts of programming, such as variables, loops, and functions. For the more experienced programmer reading the book, this chapter serves as an introduction to Lua's syntax.

Chapter 3, *Tables and Objects*, states that the most powerful features of Lua are its table and meta-table systems. Through these systems, the language it self can be extended. This chapter focuses on exploring what tables are, how they work, and how they can be used to extend the language to support concepts such as object-oriented programming.

Chapter 4, *Lua Libraries*, explains that Lua ships with a large and mature standard library. This chapter explores the functionality provided by the standard Lua libraries. The functionality exposed by the standard libraries allows us to do complicated math, work with files, and interface with the operating system.

Chapter 5, *Debugging Lua*, explains that Lua provides us with powerful debugging facilities that allow us to debug Lua code using Lua its-self. This chapter explores how to do this. In addition to exploring Lua's built-in debug facilities, optional tools that offer an intuitive and standard debugging interface are covered.

Chapter 6, *Embedding Lua*, discusses Lua's C API. This chapter covers all the API functions required to embed Lua into an existing application. Lua was designed to be an embeddable language, and therefore the C API is small, clean, and straightforward. By the end of the chapter, you will have mastered the Lua stack and will be able to work with Lua from C.

Chapter 7, *Lua Bridge*, explains that even though Lua's C API is simple, it's verbose. Doing basic tasks can take a lot of typing. Lua Bridge is a third-party Lua binding library that aims to make embedding Lua in C much easier and less verbose. All the Lua Bridge functionality needed for common tasks such as exposing functions, variables, or objects are covered in this chapter.

Chapter 8, *Next Steps*, explains that by now, you will have a solid grasp of the basics of programming, Lua, and the Lua C API. This chapter focuses on what you can do with all this new-found knowledge. Further books and learning resources are provided in this chapter. In addition to learning resources, some practical suggestions such as Lua-powered game engines and games that can be modified with Lua are made.

To get the most out of this book

- This book assumes that the reader is proficient in using a computer running either Windows, macOS, or Linux.
- For chapters one to five, no assumptions are made about the readers' programming knowledge or experience.
- Chapters six and seven assume beginner to novice familiarity with C or C++.

Download the example code files

You can download the example code files for this book from your account at `www.packtpub.com`. If you purchased this book elsewhere, you can visit `www.packtpub.com/support` and register to have the files emailed directly to you.

You can download the code files by following these steps:

1. Log in or register at `www.packtpub.com`.
2. Select the **SUPPORT** tab.
3. Click on **Code Downloads & Errata**.
4. Enter the name of the book in the **Search** box and follow the onscreen instructions.

Once the file is downloaded, please make sure that you unzip or extract the folder using the latest version of:

- WinRAR/7-Zip for Windows
- Zipeg/iZip/UnRarX for Mac
- 7-Zip/PeaZip for Linux

The code bundle for the book is also hosted on GitHub at `https://github.com/PacktPublishing/Lua-Quick-Start-Guide`. In case there's an update to the code, it will be updated on the existing GitHub repository.

We also have other code bundles from our rich catalog of books and videos available at `https://github.com/PacktPublishing/`. Check them out!

Download the color images

We also provide a PDF file that has color images of the screenshots/diagrams used in this book. You can download it here: `http://www.packtpub.com/sites/default/files/downloads/LuaQuickStartGuide_ColorImages.pdf`.

Code in Action

Visit the following link to check out videos of the code being run:
`http://bit.ly/2AawDX5`

Conventions used

There are a number of text conventions used throughout this book.

`CodeInText`: Indicates code words in text, database table names, folder names, filenames, file extensions, pathnames, dummy URLs, user input, and Twitter handles. Here is an example: "Mount the downloaded `WebStorm-10*.dmg` disk image file as another disk in your system."

A block of code is set as follows:

```
html, body, #map {
  height: 100%;
  margin: 0;
  padding: 0
}
```

When we wish to draw your attention to a particular part of a code block, the relevant lines or items are set in bold:

```
[default]
exten => s,1,Dial(Zap/1|30)
exten => s,2,Voicemail(u100)
exten => s,102,Voicemail(b100)
exten => i,1,Voicemail(s0)
```

Any command-line input or output is written as follows:

```
$ mkdir css
$ cd css
```

Bold: Indicates a new term, an important word, or words that you see onscreen. For example, words in menus or dialog boxes appear in the text like this. Here is an example: "Select **System info** from the **Administration** panel."

Warnings or important notes appear like this.

 Tips and tricks appear like this.

Get in touch

Feedback from our readers is always welcome.

General feedback: Email feedback@packtpub.com and mention the book title in the subject of your message. If you have questions about any aspect of this book, please email us at questions@packtpub.com.

Errata: Although we have taken every care to ensure the accuracy of our content, mistakes do happen. If you have found a mistake in this book, we would be grateful if you would report this to us. Please visit www.packtpub.com/submit-errata, selecting your book, clicking on the Errata Submission Form link, and entering the details.

Piracy: If you come across any illegal copies of our works in any form on the Internet, we would be grateful if you would provide us with the location address or website name. Please contact us at copyright@packtpub.com with a link to the material.

If you are interested in becoming an author: If there is a topic that you have expertise in and you are interested in either writing or contributing to a book, please visit authors.packtpub.com.

Reviews

Please leave a review. Once you have read and used this book, why not leave a review on the site that you purchased it from? Potential readers can then see and use your unbiased opinion to make purchase decisions, we at Packt can understand what you think about our products, and our authors can see your feedback on their book. Thank you!

For more information about Packt, please visit packtpub.com.

Introduction to Lua
1

This chapter covers what Lua is and how to set up a Lua environment on any operating system. Lua is not tied to any operating system, so this chapter covers installing Lua for Windows, macOS, and Linux. By the end of this chapter, you will have a fully functional Lua development environment set up, regardless of what operating system you are using. This will leave you ready to start learning the Lua language.

This is what you will learn in this chapter:

- What Lua is
- How to install Lua
- Available Lua tools
- How to install Visual Studio Code
- How to use Visual Studio Code
- Write and run a Hello World Lua application

Technical requirements

You will be required to have JavaScript programming language. Finally, to use the Git repository of this book, the user needs to install Git.

The code files of this chapter can be found on GitHub:
https://github.com/PacktPublishing/Lua-Quick-Start-Guide/tree/master/Chapter01

Check out the following video to see the code in action:
http://bit.ly/2NGKDty

What Lua is

Lua is a powerful, fast, lightweight, embeddable scripting language. The Lua virtual machine and interpreter are written in C. As a language, Lua is easy to learn. It contains 21 keywords, which makes the language rather small. Lua is also easy to read and understand, as its syntax makes it similar to English. For example, consider the following code snippet:

```
if not hero:IsAlive() then
  GameOver();
end
```

This code is easy to read, and I bet you can take an intuitive guess at what it does. Lua is not only easy to read, it is also very powerful. The real power of Lua comes from its extensible nature. Programming constructs such as **object-oriented programming (OOP)** can be implemented in Lua, even though the language has no native support for objects.

At the time of writing, Lua has 14 versions; this book will focus on **Lua 5.2.4**. The latest version is 5.3; the main difference between 5.2 and 5.3 is that 5.3 contains support for explicit integers and bitwise operation.

While this book covers everything needed to get started with Lua programming, it never hurts to have more resources. The first edition of *Programming In Lua* can be read online, for free, at https://www.lua.org/ pil/contents.html.

Source code and binaries

Lua is open source software published under the MIT License. You can browse Lua's source code at https://www.lua.org/source/. Additionally, you can download both the source code and reference manuals for Lua from https://www.lua.org/ftp/.

At the time of writing, no pre-built binaries are downloadable from the lua.org website. Pre-built binaries can be found on SourceForge at https://sourceforge.net/projects/ luabinaries/. In this chapter, we will be using SourceForge to download binaries for Lua.

Installing Lua on Windows 10

Follow these steps to install Lua 5.2.4 on Windows 10. These instructions are written for Windows 10, but the steps needed to install should be similar on older (and future) versions of Windows as well:

1. To download Lua 5.2.4, visit `https://sourceforge.net/projects/luabinaries/files/5.2.4/`.

2. Click on the **Tools and Executables** link.

3. On a 32-bit version of Windows, click the `lua-5.2.4_Win32_bin.zip` link to start downloading Lua. On a 64-bit version of Windows, click the `lua-5.2.4_Win64_bin.zip` link to start downloading.

4. Once the file is downloaded, unzip the file. Unzipping the downloaded file should create four new files: `lua52.dll`, `lua52.exe`, `luac52.exe`, and `wlua52.exe`.

5. Create a new folder inside `C:\Program Files`, and call this new folder `LUA`. Copy the four files you just unzipped into this directory.

6. Rename `lua52.exe` to `lua.exe`. If your Windows installation is set up to hide file extensions, rename `lua52` to `lua`:

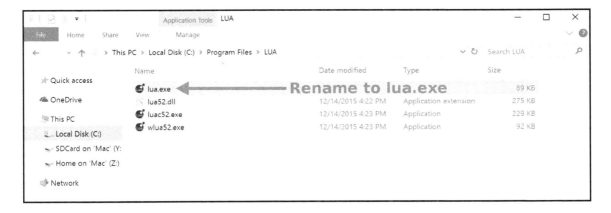

7. The path to Lua needs to be set up as an environment variable in Windows.

8. Right-click on the **Start/Windows** menu button and select the **System** option.

9. From the **System** window, select the **Advanced Settings** option.

10. Having clicked the **Advanced Settings** option, you should now see the **System Properties** dialog. In this dialog, click on the **Environment Variables...** button.

11. In the **Environment Variables** window, with the **Path** variable selected, click the **Edit...** button:

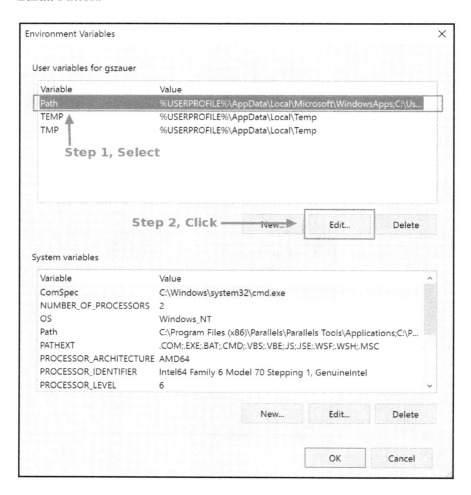

12. Inside the **Edit environment Variable** window, click the **New** button and add `C:\Program Files\LUA` as a new path. Click the **OK** button to save changes and close this window. You can close all the windows we have opened up to this point.

13. Lua should now be successfully installed on your computer. To verify the installation, you need to launch a new Command Prompt. You can launch Command Prompt by right-clicking the Windows **Start/Windows** button and selecting the **Command Prompt** item.

14. In the newly opened Command Prompt, type `lua -v`. If everything is set up correctly, the command should print out the installed version of Lua (5.2.4):

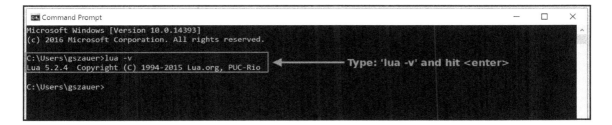

Installing Lua on macOS

Follow these steps to install Lua 5.2.4 on macOS. These instructions are written for macOS High Sierra, but the steps are the same on previous (and future) versions of macOS as well:

1. To download Lua 5.2.4, visit `https://sourceforge.net/projects/luabinaries/files/5.2.4/`.

2. Click on the **Tools and Executables** link.

3. Click on the `lua-4.2.4_MacOS1011_bin.tar.gz` link to start downloading Lua.

4. Once the zip file has downloaded, unzip it. The archive should contain two files, `lua52` and `luac52`:

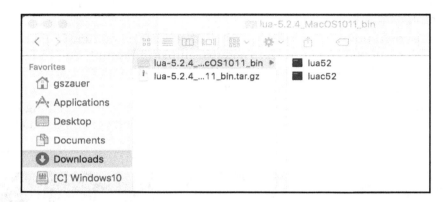

5. Create a new folder in your `~/Documents` directory, and name this folder LUA. Move both `lua52` and `luac52` into this new directory:

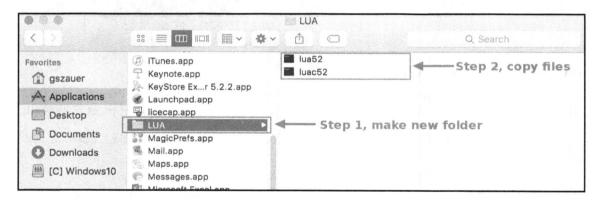

6. Rename `lua52` to just `lua`.
7. Launch a Terminal window. The Terminal app is located at `/Applications/Utilities/Terminal.app`. You can also simply type `Terminal` into the universal search on macOS.

8. With the new Terminal window open, type `sudo nano /etc/paths` and hit *Enter*. You will be asked for your password; this is the password for your user account. The password will not show up as you type it. After the password is entered, nano will open; nano is a Terminal-based text editor. You should see something similar to the following window:

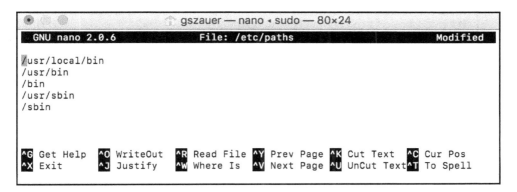

9. You can navigate the type cursor with the arrow keys. Don't worry if your `paths` file (the file we are editing) already has text in it. We will be adding a new entry into this file; where in the file you add the new entry does not matter. On a new line, type `~Documents/LUA`:

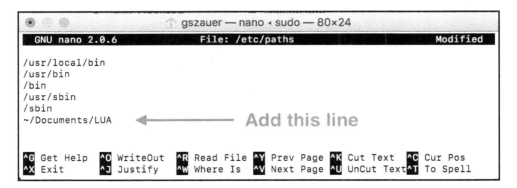

10. Press *Ctrl* + *X* to exit nano. The program will ask you if you want to save the changes you have made to the file. Press **Y** to save changes.

11. Nano will ask you to confirm the filename. Just hit *Enter* to accept the default path.

12. In order for the changes made in the paths to take effect, you must restart the Terminal app. To do this, right-click on the Terminal icon in your macOS dock and select **Quit**. Then, launch a new Terminal window.

13. In the new Terminal window, type `lua -v`. If everything is set up correctly, the Terminal should print out the installed version of Lua (5.2.4):

```
●  ●  ●                    gszauer — -bash — 80×24
Last login: Thu May 17 11:31:53 on ttys000
macbook-pro-4:~ gszauer$ lua -v
Lua 5.2.4  Copyright (C) 1994-2015 Lua.org, PUC-Rio
macbook-pro-4:~ gszauer$ 
```

Installing Lua on Linux

Follow these steps to install Lua 5.2.4 on Linux. These instructions are written for Ubuntu Linux 16.04. The steps needed to install Lua are the same on Ubuntu Linux 12.04 and higher:

1. The entire installation of Lua can be done using the command line, with the `apt` package manager.

2. Open up a new Terminal and type `sudo apt-get install lua5.2`:

```
❌ ➖ ▢   parallels@ubuntu: ~
parallels@ubuntu:~$ sudo apt-get install lua5.2
```

3. Provide your password when prompted and wait for the installation to finish:

```
😣😐😑  parallels@ubuntu: ~
File Edit View Search Terminal Help
parallels@ubuntu:~$ sudo apt-get install lua5.2
[sudo] password for parallels:
Reading package lists... Done
Building dependency tree
Reading state information... Done
The following NEW packages will be installed:
  lua5.2
0 upgraded, 1 newly installed, 0 to remove and 149 not upgraded.
Need to get 95.6 kB of archives.
After this operation, 349 kB of additional disk space will be used.
Get:1 http://us.archive.ubuntu.com/ubuntu xenial/main amd64 lua5.2 amd64 5.2.4-1
ubuntu1 [95.6 kB]
Fetched 95.6 kB in 0s (245 kB/s)
Selecting previously unselected package lua5.2.
(Reading database ... 205222 files and directories currently installed.)
Preparing to unpack .../lua5.2_5.2.4-1ubuntu1_amd64.deb ...
Unpacking lua5.2 (5.2.4-1ubuntu1) ...
Processing triggers for man-db (2.7.5-1) ...
Setting up lua5.2 (5.2.4-1ubuntu1) ...
update-alternatives: using /usr/bin/lua5.2 to provide /usr/bin/lua (lua-interpre
ter) in auto mode
update-alternatives: using /usr/bin/luac5.2 to provide /usr/bin/luac (lua-compil
er) in auto mode
parallels@ubuntu:~$
```

4. Type `lua -v`. If everything is set up correctly, the Terminal should print out the installed version of Lua (5.2.4):

```
😣😐😑  parallels@ubuntu: ~
File Edit View Search Terminal Help
parallels@ubuntu:~$ lua -v
Lua 5.2.4  Copyright (C) 1994-2015 Lua.org, PUC-Rio
parallels@ubuntu:~$ ▮
```

Tools for Lua

A programming language relies heavily on the tools that support it. Lua files are plain text files. This means you can write Lua in any text editor you want, whether it is emacs, vi, Sublime Text, TextWrangler, or just the OS-provided basic text editor.

Because of the popularity of Lua, several IDEs, such as ZeroBrane Studio, Decoda, and LuaEdit, have been created for the language. An **IDE** is an **integrated development environment**. An IDE comes with everything you need to write, compile, and execute code. There are a number of advanced text editors that have varying levels of support for Lua:

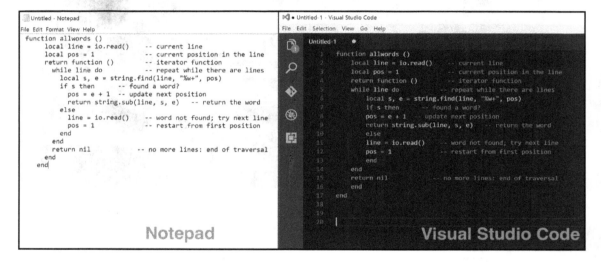

Throughout this book, we will be using Visual Studio Code. VS Code is a free text editor, which supports the Lua syntax with its default installation and works across multiple platforms. The version of VS Code used is 1.9.1, but future versions should work more or less the same way.

Installing VS Code on Windows 10

Setting up VS Code for Windows is very straightforward. The installer takes care of everything for you. These instructions are written for Windows 10, but the process should be the same on all versions of Windows:

1. Go to `http://code.visualstudio.com/` and download the VS Code Code installer for Windows.

2. Once downloaded, launch the installer exe file. The default options are all valid, so you can hit **Next** all the way through the installer.

3. Wait for the installer to finish the setup and exit the installer. There are no further actions to take.

Installing VS Code on macOS

These instructions are written for OSX High Sierra, but the installation steps should be the same on all supported versions of OSX:

1. Go to `http://code.visualstudio.com/` and download VS Code for macOS. This will download a zipped file named `VSCode-darwin-stable.zip`.

2. Double-click the zip file to extract its contents. Drag the resulting `Visual Studio Code.app` file into your `Applications` directory.

3. Once `Visual Studio Code` is in the Applications directory, it is installed, and there are no further actions to take.

Installing VS Code on Linux

These instructions are written for Ubuntu Linux 16.04. The steps needed to install Lua are the same for Ubuntu Linux 12.04 and higher.

1. Go to `http://code.visualstudio.com/` and download the Visual Studio Code installer `.deb` file. Take note of the name of the downloaded file; the version I am using is named `code_1.9.1-1486597190_amd64.deb`.

2. Once downloaded, launch a new Terminal window. Navigate the Terminal to the `downloads` folder with the following command: `cd ~/Downloads`.

3. Next, install the `.deb` file with the following command: `sudo dpkg -i ./code_1.9.1-1486597190_amd64.deb`. The filename might be different based on the version of VS Code you downloaded.

4. Fix any missing or broken dependencies with the following command: `sudo apt-get install -f`.

5. Visual Studio Code is now installed, and there are no further actions to take.

Exploring VS Code

It's important to be familiar with the tools you use. While Visual Studio Code is primarily a text editor, it does boast a rather large set of IDE-like features. VS Code can easily become overwhelming if you are not familiar with using it.

Visual Studio Code is a powerful text editor with many advanced features. If you are interested in learning more about the editor than this section covers, visit the online basics guide at `https://code.visualstudio.com/docs/editor/codebasics`.

Follow these steps to gain some familiarity and intuition with Visual Studio Code:

1. When you open up Visual Studio Code, you are greeted with either the last open documents, the welcome page, or if you have no documents open and the welcome page is disabled, the default window.
2. The icons on the left side of the screen make up what is called the View bar. Clicking any of the items on the View bar will cause a side bar to become visible:

3. The first item on the View bar is the **Explorer**. You can use the Explorer to open a folder and View all of the files in that folder in one convenient list. We will use this feature of the editor throughout the next few chapters:

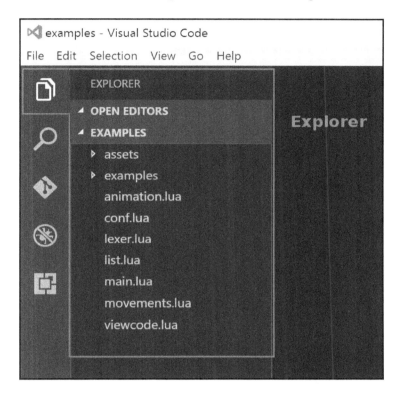

4. The search item on the bar will let you search for and replace text in either open documents, or documents inside of the currently open folder.

5. The **GIT** item on the View bar will only be available if the currently open folder is a git repository. VS Code has excellent git integration! While source control solutions such as git are outside the scope of this book, using some kind of source control is highly recommended:

6. The **DEBUG** sidebar gives VS Code IDE features such as break points and a watch window:

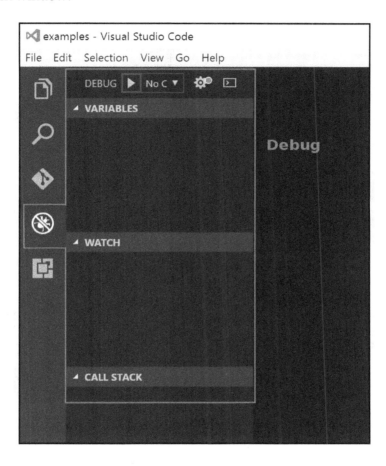

7. Finally, the **EXTENSIONS** item will show you a side bar that can be used to View, manage, and install new extensions in Visual Studio Code:

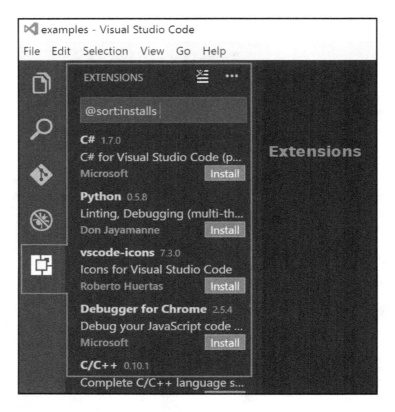

8. To make a new file, simply select **File** > **New File**.
9. This opens a new file, in a new tab. This file has no syntax highlighting yet. To assign a syntax, click on the **Plain Text** label in the bottom-right of the code tab, then select **Lua (lua)** from the drop-down menu that appears:

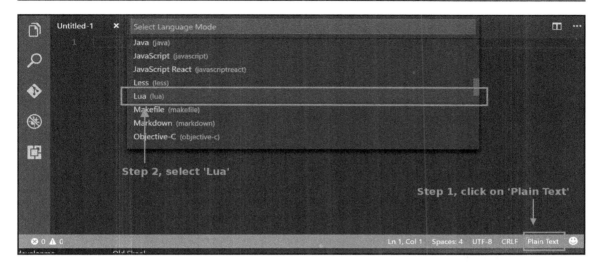

10. If at any point you open a file and it does not have proper syntax highlighting, you can follow the previous step to force the file to have Lua syntax highlighting. In the previous step, we set the syntax of the file manually. If you save a file with a `.lua` extension, the next time the file is opened, it will automatically use Lua syntax highlighting.

Hello World!

It is common practice when first learning a new programming language to create a Hello World program. This is a simple program that prints the words `Hello World` to the screen. The goal of this exercise is to write, compile (or interpret), and run a simple piece of code to prove that you can execute it.

The program will be written using Visual Studio Code, but how will it be executed? Visual Studio Code provides an Integrated Terminal. This is a Terminal that should work the same way regardless of what operating system you are using. It's important to note that whatever code gets executed through this Terminal can also be executed through the operating system Terminal/shell.

Being able to perform the same steps regardless of operating system can save time and reduce errors. For this reason, future chapters will assume code will be executed in VS Code instead of the native Terminal of each operating system.

 The Lua interpreter was set up as a global command in the console of your operating system. You should be able to execute any Lua file with the command `lua` from a console/Terminal.

Follow these steps to create a Hello World program, save it, and execute it on any platform (macOS, Windows 10, or Linux):

1. Open Visual Studio Code and make a new document with **File** > **New**.
2. Set the syntax highlighting of this file to the Lua syntax. Click on the **Plain Text** label in the bottom right of the code tab, then select **Lua (lua)** from the drop-down menu that appears:

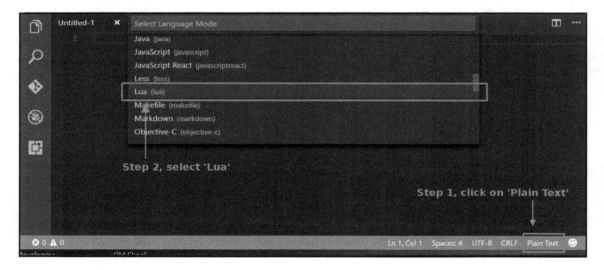

3. In this new file, type `print ('hello, world'):`

4. Save the file to your desktop and name it `hello.lua`.
5. From the top menu of Visual Studio Code, select **View > Integrated Terminal**.
6. On all platforms, if you did not have a folder open, the editor starts out in your home directory. If you did have a folder open, the editor starts out in the folder. Navigate to your desktop with the following command: `cd ~/Desktop`; the `~/` part of the path is shorthand for home directory:

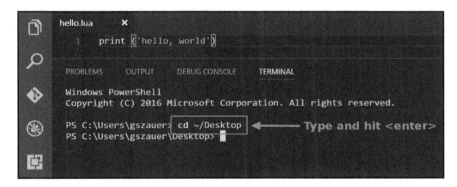

7. Now that the Terminal has the desktop directory open (which is where `hello.lua` should be saved), you can execute the Lua file with the following command: `lua hello.lua`. You should see `hello, world` printed to the Terminal.

The last step invoked the Lua binary from the Terminal of Visual Studio with the `hello.lua` file as an argument. This, in turn, launched the Lua runtime, which executed the file that was provided as an argument. If the Lua runtime did not launch, you may want to review how to set the runtime up in the *Tools for Lua* section.

Summary

This chapter covered how to install Lua and VS Code. VS Code is the development environment that will be used throughout this book to write and execute Lua code. The integrated Terminal in Visual Studio Code allows us to execute code the same way on all three major platforms: Windows, Linux, and macOS.

In the next chapter, we will start to write code. The basics of Lua, such as variables, loops, `if` statements, and functions, will be covered. The topics covered in the next chapter are the basics of programming; it is going to be one of the most important chapters in this book.

2
Working with Lua

In Chapter 1, *Introduction to Lua*, you learned how to set up Lua and Visual Studio Code. At the end of the chapter, we created a simple Hello World application. In this chapter, you will learn the basics of Lua programming. Topics such as variables, function data types, and loops are all going to be covered. By the end of this chapter, you should be familiar enough with Lua as a language to put together some simple programs.

 If this is your first time programming, the syntax of Lua can get overwhelming fast. Many resources can be found on the official Lua site at https://www.lua.org/. For a quick example of Lua, check out http://tylerneylon.com/a/learn-lua/.

By the end of this chapter, you will will have a solid understanding of the following:

- Using variables
- Data types
- Working with functions
- Operators
- Code blocks
- Variable scope
- Code flow

Technical requirements

You will be required to have JavaScript programming language. Finally, to use the Git repository of this book, the user needs to install Git.

The code files of this chapter can be found on GitHub:
https://github.com/PacktPublishing/Lua-Quick-Start-Guide/tree/master/Chapter02

Check out the following video to see the code in action:
`http://bit.ly/2LDVPd0`

Variables

Variables are labels that provide a descriptive name for some data that a program can read or modify. You can literally think of a variable as a label.

For example, let's assume there are a number of jars containing different colored jam. How do you know what flavor a specific jar contains? Hopefully, there is a label on the jar that is descriptive of its content.

The labels on the jar can change over time. For example, a jar might contain strawberry jam, but after that's gone it might be filled with peach jam. When the contents of the jar changes, a different label can be used to describe what's in it. Variables work in a similar fashion.

Creating variables

To create a variable, you need to do two things:

- Declare the variable
- Assign a value (data) to the variable

As an example, let's make a variable, `foo`, and assign it the value `bar`. The code to do this would be:

```
foo = "bar"
```

That single line of code declares a variable and assigns a string value to the variable. If you break it into several parts, the actual line of code consists of the following pieces:

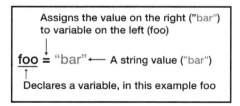

Why are there quote marks around bar? What is a string value? These questions will be answered in the coming two sections, *Basic types* and *String types*.

Printing variables

How can you tell what the value of a variable is? One way is to print the value out to the console. To print the value of a variable, you first type the keyword `print`, then the name of the variable between parentheses `()`. The full syntax is:

```
print (<variable>)
```

For example, we can check the value assigned to foo with the following code:

```
foo = "bar"
print (foo)
```

The first line of code creates a variable named `foo` and assigns it the string value `"bar"`. The second line prints the value of the foo variable. This means bar will be printed to the console:

```
Windows PowerShell
Copyright (C) Microsoft Corporation. All rights reserved.

PS C:\Users\gszauer> cd ~/Desktop
PS C:\Users\gszauer\Desktop> lua test.lua
bar
PS C:\Users\gszauer\Desktop> 
```

 Where does the `print` keyword come from? What's a keyword? Why do we use parentheses when using print? These questions will be answered in the *Functions* section of this chapter.

Assigning variables

Since a variable is just a description of the underlying data, the data can change. For example, if you have a variable named time, you would expect its value to change every second. At any point, you can use the assignment operator = to assign a new value to a variable.

This code snippet explores this by creating a single variable, color, and assigning it three different values. The value of color is printed after each assignment:

```
color = "red"
print (color)
color = "green"
print (color)
color = "blue"
print (color)
```

The output from this program should look like this:

```
Windows PowerShell
Copyright (C) Microsoft Corporation. All rights reserved.

PS C:\Users\gszauer> cd ~/Desktop
PS C:\Users\gszauer\Desktop> lua test.lua
red
green
blue
PS C:\Users\gszauer\Desktop>
```

Comments

In Lua, any time you see --, the rest of that line is considered a comment. Comments are there to help you read and understand code, but they are never executed. This example demonstrates how comments are used:

```
foo = "bar"
-- print (foo)
-- The above statement never prints
-- because it is commented out.
```

Basic types

In the last section, you were introduced to the concepts of a variable and a value. This section explores the concept of what a value is. Every value has a data type, which intuitively describes what kind of data the value holds. Lua supports eight basic value types:

- **nil**: The absence of data. This type represents literal nothingness. If a certain piece of data is invalid or unknown, nil is usually the best way to represent that it is invalid or unknown.
- **Boolean**: A value of true or false. A Boolean value is binary and can only ever be in one of two states, true or false.
- **number**: A number can represent any real number: 0, -1, 5, or even decimals such as 3.14159265359.
- **string**: A string is an array of characters. When declaring a string literal, it must be "enclosed within quotation marks."
- **function**: A function is some code that is referred to by a name and can be executed any time.
- **table**: A table contains information using key-value pairs. Tables will be covered in depth in Chapter 3, *Tables and Objects*.
- **userdata**: Complex data structures defined in the C programming language.
- **thread**: Threads can be used to execute code in parallel. Instead of your code running one set of commands, it can run several sets of commands at the same time.

This section will explore the *nil, Boolean,* and *number types*. The string and function types will get their own sections in this chapter. The table type is so important it will have its own chapter.

 Lua uses loose, implicit types. That means a variable can have any type. Once a variable is assigned a type, it can be assigned any other type. For example, it is valid to assign a number to a variable that holds a string. After the assignment, the variable will simply hold a number.

nil

A `nil` value represents the absence of data. If you try to access a variable that has not been created yet, its value will be `nil`. If you are done using a variable, you should assign it to be `nil`. This code first prints `nil` because nothing is assigned to the variable `foo`. Then, the string `bar` is assigned, and after this the code prints bar. Finally, `nil` is assigned back to the variable. The last time the variable is printed, it will print `nil` again:

```
print (foo)  -- will print: nil
foo = "bar"
print (foo)  -- will print: bar
foo = nil
print (foo)  -- will print: nil
```

Boolean

A `boolean` variable can have one of two values: true or false. Booleans are often used to control the flow of code and express logic. This code assigns the Boolean value of `true` to the variable `foo`, then prints this value:

```
foo = true
print ("The value of foo is:")
print (foo)
```

A more useful example of a Boolean is to obtain it from some kind of logical operation, for example, to check whether five is greater than three or not. This code demonstrates how to do this:

```
result = 5 > 3
print ("Is 5 > 3?")
print (result)
```

number

Lua does not know the difference between a whole number and a decimal. All numbers are simply real numbers. Sometimes, especially when working with grids, you might need only whole numbers. If that is the case, Lua has a built-in function to round down, `math.floor`, or to round up, `math.ceil`. This is how they can be used:

```
pi = 3.1415
three = math.floor(3.1415)
five = math.ceil(4.145)
```

```
print (pi) -- will print: 3.1415
print (three) -- will print: 3
print (five) -- will print: 5
```

 Using functions might look foreign right now, but don't worry, they will be covered in detail later in the chapter.

Basic arithmetic operations such as adding, subtracting, multiplying, or dividing can be performed on integers. We will cover arithmetic operations in detail later on in the chapter, but for now, let's take a look at something simple, adding two numbers:

```
five = 3 + 2
print (five) -- will print 5
print (2 + 2) -- will print 4
print (five + 1) -- will print 6
```

Finding a type

There is one very important function built into Lua, `type`. This function will return the type of a variable as a string. Let's take a look at this function in action:

```
var1 = true
var2 = 3.145
var3 = nil
var4 = type(var1)
var5 = type(type(var2))

print (type(var1)) -- boolean
print (type(var2)) -- number
print (type(var3)) -- nil
print (var4) -- boolean
print (var5) -- string
```

Because the `type` function returns a string, the result can be assigned to a variable, like so:

```
var4 = type(var1)
```

Or, the result can be passed directly to a function such as `print`, like so:

```
print (type(var1))
```

The type of the type of something `type(type(var2))`, as represented by `var5`, will always be a `string`. This is because, as stated before, `type` returns a string.

String types

A string is an array of characters. Strings can represent words, sentences, or even whole books. In this section, we will cover how to perform the following string operations:

- How to get the length of a string
- How to concatenate two strings into a single new string
- The coercion of other types into strings
- String escape characters

Additionally, this section will cover how to read input from the console. You already know how to print information to the console; applications will become much more interactive once you can also read input from the console.

String literals

A string literal must be written between quotes. The following line of code demonstrates a string literal. This example does not do anything since the literal is a value that is never assigned to a variable:

```
"hello, world"
```

Without being assigned to a variable, this string can't be printed. String literals don't have to be assigned to a variable to be useful; they can be passed directly to a function such as print. The following code demonstrates both of these cases:

```
print ("Print a string literal, used in place")
message = "Print a string assigned to a variable"
print(message)
```

String length

There are two ways to get the length of a string, either using the string.len() function, or by placing a # symbol in front of the string. Both methods work the same way, and they both return a number value. This number can be assigned to a variable or used in its place. You can call either method on a variable, or directly on a string. The following code demonstrates all of these concepts:

```
hello = "hello, world"
-- Assign length to variables
count_hash = #hello;
```

```
count_func = string.len(hello)
print ("The string:")
print (hello)
-- Print the variables assigned at the top
print ("Has a length of:")
print (count_hash)
print(count_func)
-- Use string literals, in place
print (#"hello, world")
print (string.len("hello, world"))
```

Concatenate strings

Two strings can be concatenated by placing a .. symbol between them. It is very important to have at least one space on both the left and right of the .. symbol. Concatenating two strings results in a new string, which can be stored in a variable or used in its place. Any combination of variables and literals can be concatenated, as the following code demonstrates:

```
name = "Mike"
color = "Blue"
-- Concatenate three strings
print ("Jill " .. "likes" .. " Red")
-- Concatenate a variable and a strings
print ("Jack dislikes " .. color)
-- Concatenate two variables and a string
print (name .. " likes " .. color)
-- Concatenate only variables
print (name .. color)
-- Assign result to variable
message = name .. " likes " .. color
print (message)
```

String coercion

String coercion is a fancy way of asking Lua to automatically convert data types to string representations of the data. For example, a string and an integer can be combined to form a new string like the following:

```
pi = 3.14
message = "The rounded value of pi is: " .. pi
print(message)
print("Nine: " .. 9)
```

String coercion also works the other way around! Adding a string that contains only numbers to a number is valid addition:

```
eleven = "10" + 1
print (eleven)
print (7 + "01")  -- 8
```

Escape characters

Strings need to be within quotes, but what happens when you need to put quotes inside the string? Lua doesn't care if a string uses single or double quotes, so long as the symbol at the start and end of the string matches, so technically this code would be valid:

```
message = 'he said "bye" and left'
print (message)
```

However, this is not desirable. As a convention, only double quotes will be used to represent a string throughout this book. To include a double quote within a string, the character must be escaped. Escaping a character means the character will be treated as part of the string, rather than a Lua instruction. To escape a character, place a \ in front of it, like so:

```
message = "he said \"bye\" and left"
print (message)
```

There are actually several escape characters that can be used when working with strings. The most often used escape characters are:

- \n: Newline, moves the cursor down one line
- \t: Horizontal tab, tabs over on the current line
- \\: Backslash, you have to escape the escape symbol
- \": Double quote, needed to include a quote in a string

 The full list of supported escape symbols for Lua can be found online at https://www.lua.org/pil/2.4.html.

Console input

Doing interesting things with code usually requires some kind of input from a user. Input from the console can be obtained with the `io.read()` function. Unlike the functions used previously, nothing goes inside the parentheses of this one. The function will read one line of input from the user when the user presses *Enter*. The function returns this line of text as a string, which can be stored in a variable. The following example demonstrates this:

```
print ("Please enter your name:")
name = io.read()
print ("Hello " .. name)
```

Scope

Like many other programming languages, Lua implements the concept of scope for anything that can be named (like a variable). A scope defines where in the program a variable can be used. Scopes are limited to the chunks they appear in. A chunk is just a section of code. Some languages call chunks blocks because they are represented by blocks of code.

Every Lua file that is executed is a chunk. This chunk can contain other, smaller chunks. Think of it as a hierarchical relationship. Such a relationship could be visualized as follows:

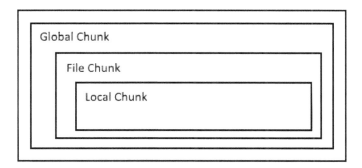

You can create a local chunk in a file by using the `do` keyword. The chunk ends with the `end` keyword. The following bit of code demonstrates how to create a local chunk in a file:

```
-- main file chunk is anywhere in the file

do
  -- local chunk
end
```

```
do
  -- a different local chunk
end
```

As mentioned earlier, scope refers to visibility. A chunk can access any variables declared in its parent chunk, but none of the variables available in any child chunks. To demonstrate this, consider the following variable declarations in different chunks:

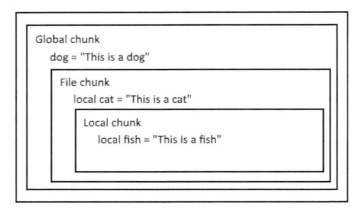

For now, ignore the syntax. In this example, the `local` chunk can see the variables `dog`, `cat`, and `fish`. However, the file chunk cannot see the `fish` variable, only `dog` and `cat`. Similarly, the global chunk can only see the `dog` variable. This diagram would be expressed in code like so:

```
-- Dog is accessible in the global chunk
dog = "This is a dog"

-- Cat is accessible in the file chunk
-- The local keyword makes cat local to the file
local cat = "This is a cat"

do -- Do / end will be discussed next
    -- Fish is in a local chunk, in this example
    -- that means local to the do/end block
    local fish = "This is a fish"
end
```

More information on scope as it refers to computer science can be found online at http://lua-users.org/wiki/ScopeTutorial.

Lua supports a few different types of chunk; this section will explore the do/end chunk properties in detail.

Scope access

Chunks are all about scope! You can access any variable defined outside of a scope from within the scope. Think of a scope like a one-way window in a room; from the inside you can see out, but from the outside you can't see in:

```
foo = 7 -- global scope
do
    local bar = 8 -- local scope
    print ("foo: " .. foo)
    print ("bar: " .. bar)
end
```

However, you can't access a variable local to a scope outside of that scope:

```
foo = 7 -- global
do
    local bar = 8 -- local
end
print ("foo: " .. foo)
print ("bar: " .. bar) -- error!
-- bar was declared local to the do/end chunk
-- it is trying to be printed at the file or
-- global chunk level, where it does not exist
```

The same access pattern is also true for multiple nested chunks:

```
foo = 7 -- global
do
    local bar = 8 -- local
    do
      local x = 9 -- nested local
      -- can access foo, bar and x
    end
    -- can access foo and bar
end
-- can only access foo
```

Global scope

Notice in the last few examples the use of the `local` keyword. If you omit the local keyword, the variable is considered to be in global scope. Without the local keyword, the variable is global, no matter what chunk it is in:

```
foo = 7 -- global
do
    bar = 8 -- global
end
print ("foo: " .. foo)
print ("bar: " .. bar)
```

The global scope is interesting. It is not tied directly to a Lua file. The `local` keyword can be used outside any `do/end` chunks to make a variable local to the file it is loaded from:

```
foo = 7 -- global, can be accesssed from any loaded lua file
local x = 9 -- local to the .lua file being executed
do
    local bar = 8 -- local to the current do/end chunk
end
```

Shadowing

You can give a variable local to a chunk the same name as a global variable. If you were to do this, then print the variable inside the chunk, what would happen? The value of the variable inside the chunk would print.

This is called **variable shadowing**. If the same variable name is used in different scopes, the variable closest to the scope you are using it in will be used. The following code example demonstrates this concept:

```
message = "global-scope"
-- This should print: global-scope
print ("message: " .. message)
do
    -- Shadow the message variable
    local message = "local-scope"
    -- This print uses the variable declared
    -- in this block (shadowing). Should print: local-scope
    print ("message: " .. message)
end
```

```
-- The variable that was declared in the local scope
-- of the above block is gone. message now holds
-- the global scope again. Should print: global-scope
print ("message: " .. message)
```

Functions

A function is essentially a named chunk of code. Unlike other chunks, the contents of a function are not automatically executed when the file is loaded. When a file is first loaded, functions are simply defined. Once a function has been defined, you can execute the function by calling it. Because a function is a named chunk, you can call a function as many times as you want. The same scope rules apply to functions as to do/end blocks.

 Read more about functions online at https://www.lua.org/pil/5.html.

Defining a function

A function declaration starts with the `function` keyword. After the function keyword, you provide the **function name**. The name of the function follows the same naming rules as the name of a variable.

After the name of your function, you have to provide a list of parameters. Parameters are variable names enclosed in parentheses `()`. The list of parameters may be empty if a function needs no parameters, in which case only opening and closing parentheses are given—`()`.

Once you have declared the list of parameters, you may write the body of the function. The function body is a chunk of code, so like other chunks you need to close the body with the end keyword. The following code demonstrates a simple function:

```
function PrintSomething()
  text1 = "hello"
  text2 = "world"
  print (text1 .. ", " .. text2)
end
```

This function definition can be broken down into the following parts:

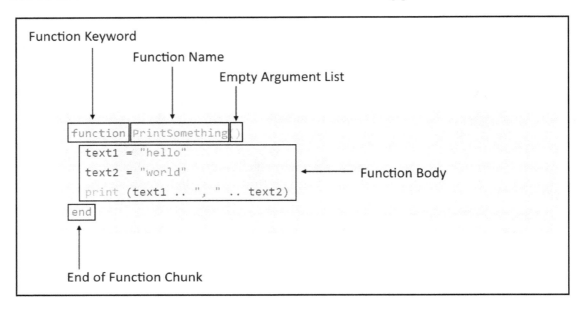

Calling a function

Once a function is declared, it can be executed by calling it. To call a function, simply type its name, followed by parentheses. For example, to read input from the console, you call `io.read()`. The following snippet demonstrates how to declare and call your own function:

```
print ('about to declare the PrintSomething function');

function PrintSomething() -- declare the function
  print ('hello, world')
end

print ('the PrintSomething function is declared');
print ('calling the PrintSomething function');

PrintSomething(); -- call the function

print ('called the PrintSomething function');
```

Function arguments

Functions can take arguments. An argument is some data that will be passed into the function. You have passed arguments to the print function before; it takes a single string argument. Calling print with an argument looks like this: `print ('hello, world')`.

When you declare a function, you can place one or more variable names inside the parentheses that are used during the function declaration. These variables are the function arguments; they have a scope local to the function.

The following function takes in two numbers and adds them together:

```
-- Declare the function, takes two arguments
function AddAndPrint(x, y)
  local result = x + y;
  print (x .. "+" .. y .. "=" .. result)
end

-- Call the function a few times
AddAndPrint(2, 3)
AddAndPrint(4, 5)
AddAndPrint(6, 7)
```

Any number of arguments

Unlike other programming languages, in Lua you don't have to provide the same number of arguments as a function's declaration has. For example, adding more arguments than is declared will simply ignore the extra arguments:

```
-- Declare the function, takes two arguments
function AddAndPrint(x, y)
  local result = x + y;
  print (x .. "+" .. y .. "=" .. result)
end

-- Call the function a few times
AddAndPrint(2, 3, 7) -- Will print 2+3=5
AddAndPrint(4, 5, 8, 9, 10) -- Will print 4+5=9
AddAndPrint(6, 7, 11, 12, 14) -- Will print 6+7=13
```

On the other hand, if you add less arguments than the declaration has, the missing variables will get a value of nil:

```
-- Declare the function, takes two arguments
function PrintValues(x, y)
  print ("x: " .. tostring(x) .. ", y: " .. tostring(y))
end

-- Call the function a few times
PrintValues(3, 4) -- will print x: 3, y: 4
PrintValues(1) -- will print x: 1, y: nil
PrintValues() -- will print x: nil, y: nil
```

In this code listing, x and y are passed to a tostring function before being concatenated to the string that will print. The tostring function is built into Lua; it needs to be called to avoid the error generated when attempting to concatenate nil to a string.

Returning a value

Functions don't just take input, they can also return some output to the calling code. This is done through a return value. When a function returns a value, it can be called as part of an expression or as a standalone statement.

If a function is called as a part of an expression, its return value can be assigned to a variable, or used wherever a variable could be used. The following code demonstrates this concept:

```
-- declare the function
function AddTwo(x)
  result = x + 2
  print (x .. " + 2 = " .. result)
  return result
end

AddTwo(3) -- calls as statement
nine = 7 + AddTwo(5) -- Call as expression
print ("adding two " .. AddTwo(3)) -- Call as expression
```

When a function hits a return statement, it returns whatever data follows and stops executing. If you have code after your return statement, that code will not execute, for example:

```
-- Declare the function
function SquareIt(number)
  result = number * number
```

```
print ("this will print") -- WILL PRINT!
do
   return result
end
print ("this will not print") -- WILL NOT PRINT
end

-- Call the function
four = SquareIt(2) -- Will print: this will print
print(four) -- Will print: 4
```

 Why is the return value inside of a do/end block? In Lua, the return keyword is only valid when followed by the end keyword. Without the do/end block around the return statement, this code would not compile, because following a return with a print statement is not valid.

Returning multiple values

Lua has a unique feature that many traditional languages don't, **multiple return values**. This feature allows one function to return multiple values. To return multiple values, assign the result of the function to a list of variables separated by commas.

For example, you could write a function that takes a number for an argument and returns both the squared and cubed values of that number:

```
-- Declare the function
function SquareAndCube(x)
   squared = x * x
   cubed = x * x * x
   return squared, cubed
end

-- Call the function
s, c = SquareAndCube(2)
print ("Squared: " .. s) -- will print: Squared: 4
print ("Cubed: " .. c) -- will print: Cubed: 8
```

Like with function arguments, the number of values a function returns does not have to match the number of variables it is assigned to. What happens if you return two values, but try to assign them to three variables? The extra variables will have a default value of nil:

```
s, c, q = SquareAndCube(2) -- Call the same function
print ("Squared: " .. s) -- will print: Squared: 4
print ("Cubed: " .. c) -- will print: Cubed: 8
print ("Quartic: " .. tostring(q)) -- will print: Quartic: nil
```

Similarly, you can return two values and try to assign them to a single variable. In this case, the first value is assigned and the rest of the variables are discarded. The following code demonstrates this:

```
square = SquareAndCube(2) -- Call the same function
-- rest of results are discarded
print ("Squared: " .. square) -- will print: Squared: 4
```

Operators

Operators such as addition +, string concatenation .., and even the assignment operator = have been used throughout this book. Let's take some time to cover in detail what operators are and how they work. Operators fall into one of the following categories:

- **Arithmetic operators** do math.
- **Relational operators** always return a Boolean value: true or false. Relational operators are used to compare the relationship between two things, for example, by checking whether one number is smaller than another number.
- **Logical operators** express complex relations such as and/or. For example, logical operations can be used to check whether a number is less than seven AND greater than two.
- **Misc operators**: All other operators, such as assignment, fall into this category.

Operators can be *unary* or *binary*. A **unary** operation works on only one operand. For example, the minus sign (–) is the unary negation operator. It returns the negative value of a number:

```
x = -7 -- negation operator applied to the constant 7
y = -x -- negation operator applied to the x variable
-- x: -7, y: 7
```

A **binary** operator on the other hand operates on two operands. The binary subtraction operator also uses the minus sign (–), but it is a completely different operator from its unary counterpart. An example of the binary subtraction operator would be:

```
x = 7 - 3 -- Operand 1 is the constant 7, Operand 2 is the constant 3
y = x - 1 -- Operand 1 is the variable x, Operand 2 is the constant 1
z = x - y -- Operand 1 is the variable x, Operand 2 is the variable y
```

Most operators will be binary, that is, they will work on two operands.

Arithmetic operators

Arithmetic operators do math; these operators work on numbers to perform addition, subtraction, multiplication, and division. Operators to find the remainder of a division, negate a number, or raise a number to a power are also available in Lua. The negation operator uses a minus sign and is a unary operator; otherwise, all other arithmetic operators are binary operators (that is, they work on two operands).

The addition operator (+) adds two operands together:

```
x = 7 + 10
y = x + 3
z = x + y
```

The subtraction operator (–) will subtract the second operand from the first:

```
x = 8 - 3
y = 10 - x
z = x - y
```

The multiplication operator (*) will multiply the given operands:

```
x = 2 * 2
y = x * 3
z = x * y
```

The division operator (/) will divide the numerator (first operand) by the denominator (second operand):

```
x = 20 / 10
y = 5 / x
z = x / y
```

The modulus operator (%) returns the remainder of an integer division. This means both the numerator (first operand) and denominator (second operand) are cast to be integers, divided, and the result is returned. Numbers are cast to integers, not rounded. This means that any decimal numbers are discarded, so 5.1, 5.5, and 5.9 would all simply become 5. Here is an example:

```
x = 5 % 2 -- result is 1
y = 5.7 % 2 -- 5.7 is treated as 5, result is 1.
z = 5.3 % 2.9 -- result is 1
```

 Why is the result of 5 % 2 simply 1? Two divides into five evenly twice, with a remainder of 1. The modulus operator returns the remainder of this division.

The negation operator (−) negates a number. This is the only unary arithmetic operator. Here is an example:

```
x = -5 -- x = -5
y = -x -- y = 5
y = -y -- y = -5
```

The exponent operator (^) will take the base (first operand) and raise it to the power of the exponent (second operand):

```
x = 10 ^ 2
y = x ^ 2
z = 3 ^ 3
```

 Lua only offers partial support for the exponent operator. An explanation of why this decision was made is available online at https://www.lua.org/pil/3.1.html.

Relational operators

Relational operators compare two things (usually numbers) and always evaluate to a Boolean result. These operators are used to answer questions such as is 10 less than 20? Relational operators test for equality, inequality, and which of two arguments is less than or greater than the other.

The equality operator (==) checks whether the values of the two operands are equal or not. If they are equal, the operator evaluates to true, otherwise it evaluates to false. Here are examples:

```
x = 2 == 2 -- true
y = 2 == 3 -- false
z = "nine" == 9 -- false
```

The inequality operator (~=) checks whether the values of the two operands are equal or not. If they are NOT equal, the operator evaluates to true, otherwise it evaluates to false. Here is an example:

```
x = 2 ~= 2 -- false
y = 2 ~= 3 -- true
z = "nine" ~= 9 -- true
```

The greater than operator (>) checks whether the first operand is greater than the second operand. If it is, the operator evaluates to true, otherwise to false. Here is an example:

```
x = 4 > 5 -- false
y = 4 > 4 -- false
z = 4 > 3 -- true
```

The greater than or equal to operator (>=) checks whether the first operand is greater than or equal to the second operand. If it is, the operator evaluates to true, otherwise to false. Here is an example:

```
x = 4 >= 5 -- false
y = 4 >= 4 -- true
z = 4 >= 3 -- true
```

The less than operator (<) checks whether the first operand is less than the second operand. If it is, the operation evaluates to true, otherwise to false. Here is an example:

```
x = 3 < 2 -- false
y = 3 < 3 -- false
z = 3 < 4 -- true
```

The less than or equal to operator (<=) checks whether the first operand is less than or equal to the second operand. If it is, the operation evaluates to true, otherwise to false. Here is an example:

```
x = 3 <= 2 -- false
y = 3 <= 3 -- true
z = 3 <= 4 -- true
```

Logical operators

Logical operators test the relationship of two statements. Logical operators work a little differently in Lua than in other languages. In Lua, anything not false is considered to be true. Only two values represent false for a logical operator, the constant value of false and nil; anything else is true.

 Logical operators in Lua do not evaluate to a Boolean result; rather they evaluate to one of the provided operands.

The and operator returns its first operand if that operand is false and the second operand if the first operand was true. Here is an example:

```
x = true and false -- value is false
y = false and false -- value is false
z = true and true -- value is true
w = 7 and 1 -- value is 1
```

The or operator (or) returns its second operand if it is not false, otherwise it will return the first operand. Here is an example:

```
x = true or false -- value is true
y = false or false -- value is false
z = true or true -- value is true
w = 7 or 1 -- value is 7
```

The and/or operators both use shortcut evaluation. This means that the second operand is only evaluated if needed. This is important when the operands are functions. Here is an example:

```
function TrueFunction()
  print ("returning true")
  return true
end

function FalseFunction()
  print ("returning false")
  return false
end

x = FalseFunction() and TrueFunction()
```

This statement only evaluates the `false` function. Only returning `false` is printed. But if we changed the line that assigns x to be the following:

```
x = TrueFunction() and FalseFunction()
```

After changing the line, both functions will evaluate, and both returning `true` and returning `false` will be printed. Shortcut evaluation can make bugs difficult to spot; for this reason, try to avoid functions as operands when using logical operators.

The logical `not` operator is a unary operator. It reverses the logical state of its operand. Provided with a value that is `false`, this operator will evaluate to `true`. Provided with a value that is `true`, the operator evaluates to `false`. Here is an example:

```
x = not true -- false
y = not true or false -- false
z = not not false -- false
w = not (7 + 1) -- false
```

Misc operators

The miscellaneous operators presented here do not fit into any of the previous groups. These operators are Lua constructs.

The assignment operator (=) changes the value of a variable. This operator has been used many times up until this point. The assignment operator allows for *multiple assignment*. All of the following are valid:

```
x = 2
y, z = 4, "hello"
```

The string concatenation operator (. .) will combine two strings into a single string. This operator was covered in the *String types* section of this chapter. As a reminder, the syntax is:

```
hello = "hello,"
world = " world"
print (hello .. world)
```

Finally, the length operator (#) is a unary operator that will return the length of a string or a table. The use of this operator for strings has already been covered. The syntax of this operator is as follows:

```
print ("Enter a word: ")
word = io.read();
print (word .. " has " .. #word .. " letters!")
```

Operator precedence

Much like math, Lua has the concept of operator precedence. In math, 5 + 2 * 10 equals 25 because multiplication happens before addition. Lua behaves the same way; it even uses parentheses to prioritize one group of equations before another. To see this in action, try running the following code snippet:

```
print ( 5 + 2 * 10 ) -- prints 25
print ( (5 + 2) * 10 ) -- prints 70
```

Take note of how the output is different; this is because Lua follows mathematical precedence for arithmetic operators. Order of precedence is listed in this table from higher priority (first row) to lower priority (last row):

^					
not	#	- (unary)			
*	/	%			
+	-				
..					
<	>	<=	>=	~=	==
and					
or					

Control structures

Control structures are used to make decisions in code; they control the path of code based on a Boolean value. Lua provides the if statement for this purpose. An if statement is followed by a Boolean condition, which in turn is followed by a then/end chunk. The chunk is only executed when the Boolean condition evaluates to true.

The most basic syntax of an if statement is as follows:

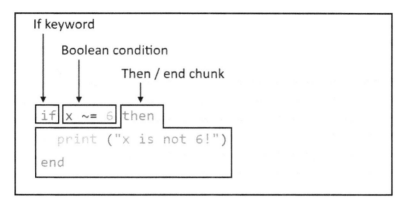

if

A logical control structure always starts with an if statement. As described previously, an `if` statement consists of the `if` keyword, a Boolean expression, and a `then/end` chunk. The then/end chunk is only executed when the Boolean condition evaluates to `true`. The following code sample demonstrates the basic use of an if statement:

```
print ("Enter your name")
name = io.read()

if #name <= 3 then
    print ("that's a short name, " .. name)
end
```

elseif

You might want to make a more complicated decision than a simple if statement allows. For example, you may want to do one thing if the length of a string is less than three, but another thing if the length of a string is greater than three AND less than six! This can be achieved with the elseif statement.

> Unlike other languages, there is no space between else and if; it's one keyword: `elseif`.

An `elseif` must always follow an `if`. Syntactically, an `elseif` statement is followed by a Boolean condition which is then followed by a `then`/`end` block. The `elseif` statement follows the body of the then block of an if statement, but goes before the `end` statement. The following code demonstrates the syntax of an `elseif` statement:

```
print ("Enter your name")
name = io.read()

if #name <= 3 then
    print ("that's a short name, " .. name)
elseif #name <= 6 then
    print (name .. " is an average length name")
end
```

You can add as many `elseif` statements to one `if` statement as you want. The following code example demonstrates this:

```
print ("Enter a number")
x = io.read()

if x == "0" then
    print ("input is 0!")
elseif x == "1" then
    print ("input is 1!")
elseif x == "2" then
    print ("input is 2!")
elseif x == "3" then
    print ("input is 3!")
end
```

else

What happens when none of the `if` or `elseif` statements evaluate to `true`? No chunk of code is executed. But, you might want some chunk of code to execute when none of the `if`/`elseif` arguments are `true`. This is what the `else` statement does. It executes a chunk of code when none of the statements tested by the preceding `if`/`elseif` tests were `true`.

Syntactically, the `else` statement is just an `else`/`end` chunk. The `else` statement always comes last, as demonstrated by the following code:

```
print ("Enter your name")
name = io.read()

if #name <= 3 then
    print ("that's a short name, " .. name)
```

```
elseif #name <= 6 then
    print (name .. " is an average length name")
else
    print ("that's a long name, " .. name)
end
```

There can be only one `else` statement, and it must be at the end of your `if/elseif` logic. An `else` does not have to follow an `elseif`; it could simply follow an `if`:

```
print ("Enter a number")
x = io.read()

if x % 2 == 0 then
    print (x .. " is even")
else
    print (x .. " is odd")
end
```

Nesting if statements

`if/elseif/else` statements control the execution of chunks of code. Like chunks, `if` statements can be nested. The same rule for scope applies to nested `if` statements as it does to nested chunks. The following code demonstrates the use of nested `if` statements:

```
print ("Enter a number")
x = io.read()

if x == "6" then
    print ("x is six!")

    print ("Enter another number")
    local y = io.read()
    -- Nested if statement begins here
    if y == "6" then
        print ("y is also six!")
    elseif y == "5" then
        print ("y is one less than x")
    else
        print ("x is 6, but y is not!")
    end
    -- Nested if statement ends here
else
    print ("x is not 6!" .. x)
end
```

Loops

A chunk of code can be repeated multiple times by using a loop. Lua provides three types of loop, the `while`, `repeat`, and `for` loops. Each loop type will be covered in depth, but the rest of the book will mainly use the for loop.

while loops

Syntactically, a while loop starts with the while keyword, followed by a Boolean condition and a do/end chunk. The loop will keep executing the chunk of code so long as the Boolean condition evaluates to `true`:

```
x = 10 -- Initialize a "control" variable

while x > 0 do -- Boolean condition: x > 0
    print ("hello, world")

    x = x - 1 -- Decrement the "control" variable
end
```

Infinite loops

One of the dangers of loops is an infinite loop. You get into an infinite loop when the condition of the loop never evaluates to false. Because the condition keeps being `true`, the loop goes on forever. The following code snippet demonstrates a simple infinite loop:

```
while true do
    print ("forever")
end
```

A more real-life example of an infinite loop would look like this:

```
x = 10 -- Initialize a "control" variable

while x > 0 do -- Boolean condition: x > 0
    print ("hello, world")

    x = x + 1 -- Decrement the "control" variable
end
```

This loop will run forever, since the value of x keeps increasing and will never reach 0.

If you encounter an infinite loop, force stop the execution of the program in any terminal with the keyboard shortcut *Ctrl + C*, which kills the current process.

Breaking a loop

A loop might need to exit mid-execution, before the loop condition could evaluate to false. Or, perhaps there is a certain branch of logic that should exit a loop in case of an error. At any point during the loop's execution, the break keyword stops the execution of a loop immediately, as the following code snippet demonstrates:

```
x = 0

while x < 10 do -- Execute 10 times!
    print ("x is " .. x)

    if x == 5 then
        -- This stops the loop execution at 5
        break
    end

    x = x + 1
end
```

This code should loop from 0 to 9 and print out the value of x at each step. However, when x is 5, the loop breaks. Because of this break, this code only outputs 0 through 5.

If you are coming to Lua from another language, you might expect to see a continue statement. Lua does not implement continue.

The return statement also breaks a loop; it also halts execution of the current function. The break statement stops the loop and executes what comes after it. The return statement on the other hand stops the entire function; the loop executing will stop and nothing in the rest of the function will execute. For example, see the following code sample:

```
function Foo() -- Declare Foo
    local x = 0
    while x < 10 do
        if x == 5 then
```

```
            break -- Stop executing the while loop
        end -- end if x == 5
        x = x + 1
    end -- end while x < 10

    -- This print statement will execute
    print ("x is " .. x)

    local y = 0
    while y < 10 do
        if y == 5 then
            return y -- Stop executing the function
        end -- end if y == 5
        y = y + 1
    end -- end while y < 10

  -- This print statement will NOT execute, because of the return statement
    print ("y is " .. y)

end -- end function Foo

-- Call the function Foo
Foo()
```

In this code, x is printed because the break statement stops the loop execution, but lets the function finish executing. However, y is not printed because the `return` statement stops the function from executing.

Repeat until loop

A repeat until loop is slightly different from a while loop. When using a while loop, the initial expression is evaluated first, so the following code would not execute the chunk of code belonging to the loop:

```
while false do
  print ("Not going to print")
end
```

This happens because the Boolean condition of the loop is evaluated before the chunk of code is executed. A repeat until loop works the opposite way. The chunk of the repeat loop is executed first, then the condition is evaluated. This guarantees that a repeat until loop will execute its chunk at least once.

Syntactically, the repeat until loop begins with the `repeat` keyword, followed by the chunk of code to loop. The chunk ends with the `until` keyword, which is followed by the logical expression to evaluate which determines if the loop should execute or not. The following piece of code demonstrates a repeat until loop that executes once but never actually loops:

```
x = 10
repeat
  print ("Repeat loop")
until x > 2
```

for loop

Lua has two flavors of the `for` loop, the numeric for and a generic for. The generic for is used to iterate over collections and will be covered in Chapter 3, *Tables and Objects*. For now, let's focus on the numeric for loop.

Syntactically, a numeric for loop consists of the `for` keyword, three expressions, and a do/end chunk. The three expressions are the **initial expression**, **final expression**, and **step expression**. Each expression is separated by a comma. The format for the loop looks like this:

```
for variable = initial_exp, final_exp, step_exp do
  -- Chunk
end
```

The result of the intial expression should be numeric; it will be assigned to a variable local to the for loop. The loop will increment or decrement this variable so long as it is not equal to the final expression. The variable is incremented or decremented by the value of the step expression.

For example, the following code loops from 0 to 10. The loop increments the counter by one on each iteration and prints out the value of the counter:

```
for i = 0, 10, 1 do
    print ( i )
end
```

You don't have to increment the loop by one every iteration. The step expression can be any number you wish. If we set the step expression to two, it will increment by 2 on each iteration:

```
for i = 0, 10, 2 do
    print ( i )
end
```

A numeric for loop does not have to count up; it can count down. To count down, set the initial expression to be greater than the final expression and the step expression to be negative. Like counting up, the step expression can be any number:

```
for i = 10, 0, -1 do
    print ( i )
end
```

Counting up by one is a very common use case for loops, so common that Lua provides a nifty shorthand for it with the for loop. If you provide only an initial expression and final expression, Lua will assume you want to count up by one and that the step expression is one:

```
for i = 0, 10 do
    print ( i )
end
```

Nested loops

Much like control structures, loops operate on a chunk of code. Also, similar to control structures, loops can be nested. You can nest different types of loops within each other. The same scope rules apply to nesting loops as to everything else so far.

If you have a break statement, it will only break one loop, the innermost loop closest to the statement. The following piece of code demonstrates breaking out of nested loops:

```
for i = 0, 10 do
    local j = 0
    while j < 10 do
        print ("j: " .. j) -- Will never be > 2
        if j == 2 then
            print ("j is: " .. j .. ", i is:" .. i)
            break
        end
        j = j + 1
    end
end
```

Summary

This chapter covered a lot of topics, such as variables, data types, functions, operators, code blocks, scope, and code flow. All of these concepts are the basic building blocks of Lua. These concepts are very important to programming, so you may need to come back to this chapter.

In Chapter 3, *Tables and Objects*, we will cover tables and objects. An alternate syntax of the for loop will be covered that can be used to easily iterate over tables or arrays.

3
Tables and Objects

The only data structure provided by Lua is the table. As discussed in `Chapter 2`, *Working with Lua*, the table is one of the built-in data types Lua provides. Tables are powerful enough to implement other data structures, such as lists, queues, or stacks.

Lua is not object-oriented; the language does not have support for objects. However, using tables and meta-tables, an object system can be implemented from the ground up. By the end of this chapter, you will have implemented an object system in Lua.

This chapter will cover the following topics:

- Introduction to tables
- Arrays
- Iterating
- Meta tables
- Objects
- Inheritance

Technical requirements

You will be required to have JavaScript programming language. Finally, to use the Git repository of this book, the user needs to install Git.

The code files of this chapter can be found on GitHub:
`https://github.com/PacktPublishing/Lua-Quick-Start-Guide/tree/master/Chapter03`

Check out the following video to see the code in action:
`http://bit.ly/2JUofdV`

Introduction to tables

Tables are the only data structure available in Lua. The table data structure is powerful enough to implement other data structures. Tables can also be used to extend the Lua language with a class system, or even a mixin system, which is an alternative to class-based composition. So, what is a table?

Tables are basically a dictionary or array. A table is a key-value pair. If the keys to the table are numeric, the table represents an array. If the keys are non-numeric or mixed, the table is a dictionary. Anything can be used as a key in a table, other than `nil`. Anything, including `nil`, can be a value.

Creating tables

A table in Lua is created with the curly brace { } symbols. After a table is created, it needs to be assigned to a variable. If you don't assign the table to a variable, you won't be able to refer to it. The following code creates a new table and assigns it to the `tbl` variable. The code then prints out the type of the `tbl` variable, which should be a table:

```
tbl = {} -- Creates table, assigns it to tbl variable
print("The type of a table is: " .. type(tbl))
```

Storing values

Tables store values; a table is a relational data structure. This makes the table similar to a dictionary in other languages. To store a variable in a table, use the following syntax:

```
table[key] = value
```

The following example demonstrates how to make a table, store a value with the key x, and how to retrieve that value:

```
tbl = {}
tbl["x"] = 20
i = "x"

print (tbl["x"])
print (tbl[i])
```

The key of a table can be any type (even another table!), except for `nil`. This makes the following code valid—hard to read, but valid:

```
tbl = {}

tbl["x"] = 10
tbl[10] = "x"

print ("x: " .. tbl["x"])
print ("10: " .. tbl[10])
```

If you use a string key for a table, you can access it with the dot syntax. This syntax allows you to access the same data, but is easier to type. The dot syntax feels more natural than braces.

The following code declares the x variable using a string key, then retrieves the value of x using a string literal, a string stored in a variable, and finally the dot syntax. Next, the sample code declares the y variable using the dot syntax:

```
tbl = {}
tbl["x"] = 20
i = "x"

print (tbl["x"])
print (tbl[i])
print (tbl.x)

tbl.y = 10

print ("x + y: " .. tbl.x + tbl.y)
print (tbl["y"])
print (tbl.y)
```

One last thing to note about storing values in tables is the default value. Just like global variables, if you don't assign a value to a key in a table, the default value is `nil`. The following code demonstrates this:

```
tbl = {}
-- z is never added to the table!
print (tostring(tbl["z"])) -- nil
print (tostring(tbl.z)) -- nil
```

Table constructor

If you know the values stored in a table at the time of creating the table, you can use the table constructor to assign the values. Just write the key/variable pairs as assignment statements between the curly braces that define the table. By not including strings, the keys are assumed to be strings:

```
colors = {
  red = "#ff0000",
  green = "#00ff00",
  blue = "#0000ff"
}

print ("red: " .. colors.red)
print ("green: " .. colors["green"])
print ("blue: " .. colors.blue)
```

Non-string keys can be used if the bracket notation is followed within the constructor. The following code shows valid ways to declare table elements in the table constructor:

```
colors = { r = "#ff0000", ["g"] = "#00ff00", [3] = "#0000ff"}

print ("red: " .. colors.r)
print ("green: " .. colors.g)
print ("blue: " .. colors[3])
```

Tables are references

The last thing to know about tables before moving on to the next section is that they are stored by reference, not value! This is very important: integers and other primitive types are assigned by value, tables are assigned by reference. What does this mean?

If you assign one variable to another variable by value, each variable has its own copy. This means you can edit both variables independently. Here is an example:

```
x = 10 -- y assigned 10 by value
y = x -- y assigned the value of x (10) by value

x = 15 -- x assigned 15 by value

print (x) -- 15
print (y) -- 10
```

When you assigned a variable by reference, however, multiple variables might hold the same reference. If you assign the same reference to multiple variables, changing one variable will change the data referenced by all variables. This can cause subtle bugs to appear in your code. The following code demonstrates this:

```
a = {} -- a is assigned a table reference
b = a -- b references the same table as x

b.x = 10 -- also creates a.x, a and b reference the same table
a.y = 20 -- also creates b.y, a and b reference the same table
a.x = 30 -- also changes b.x, a and b reference the same table

-- Even tough we assigned different variables to a.x and b.x
-- because the variables reference the same table, they should
-- both have the same value
print ("a.x: " .. a.x) -- prints a.x: 30
print ("b.x: " .. b.x) -- print b.x: 30

print ("a.y: " .. a.y) -- printx a.y: 20
print ("b.y: " .. b.y) -- prints b.y: 20

a = nil -- a no longer references the table
b = nil -- nothing references the table after this
```

Take note of the last two lines. Both variables a and b are set to `nil`. When a table is not referenced by any variable, it becomes eligible for garbage collection. Garbage collection is the mechanism in Lua by which memory is freed, so that it can be re-used later. Once a table is no longer needed, all references to that table should be made `nil`.

Arrays

An array is a contiguous chunk of memory; some programming languages guarantee that the memory will be contiguous. In Lua, an array might use a linear chunk of memory if the following apply:

- The table has only numeric indices
- The numeric indices start from one
- At least half of the indices are not nil

How tables are implemented is dependent on the internals of Lua. This is not something you usually have to concern yourself with, but if you are interested, the topic is described in detail at http://www.lua.org/doc/ jucs05.pdf.

For now, assume that an array is defined as a table that is indexed only numerically, starting with index 1. By this definition, the following code demonstrates how to use a table as an array:

```
arr = {}

arr[1] = "x"
arr[2] = "y"
arr[3] = "z"

for i = 1,3 do
    print(arr[i])
end
```

Array constructor

Tables in Lua have a constructor, which will index the table as an array. To use this constructor, you need to enter values without keys in the curly braces that create the table. The first value will be given a key of 1, and each subsequent value will have an index one higher than the last:

```
arr = { "monday", "tuesday", "wednesday" }

for i=1,3 do
    print (arr[i])
end
```

Arrays are one-based

Lua has one-based arrays. This means the language assumes that the first element of the array will occupy index 1. This is in contrast to languages such as C or Java, in which arrays start at index 0. The default array constructor places the first element of the array in index 1, as follows:

```
vector = { "x", "y", "z" }

print (tostring(vector[0])) -- nil, the array starts at 1
print (vector[1]) -- first element, x
```

```
print (vector[2]) -- second element, y
print (vector[3]) -- third element, z
```

Lua is a very forgiving language. You can absolutely assign any value to any index. This means, if you really want to, you can explicitly place a value in index 0 as follows:

```
vector = { [0] = "x", "y", "z", "w" }

print (vector[0]) -- element before first, x
print (vector[1]) -- first element, y
print (vector[2]) -- second element, z
print (vector[3]) -- third element, w
```

Putting elements in index 0, while possible, goes against Lua convention. Doing so will introduce subtle, hard-to-track bugs. An example of one of these bugs will be presented later in this section when we discuss finding the size of an array. Avoid using index 0 and stick to the Lua convention.

Sparse arrays

Arrays can be sparse, meaning an array can have a hole in it. Elements can be assigned to index 1 and 2 of an array, leaving 3 and 4 blank and then assigning elements 5 and 6. Any hole in the array will have a default value of `nil`, as the following code segment demonstrates:

```
arr = { }

arr[1] = "x"
arr[2] = "y"
-- arr[3] is nil by default
-- arr[4] is nil by default
arr[5] = "z"
arr[6] = "w"

for i=1,6 do
    print (tostring(arr[i]))
end
```

This implies that setting the value of an existing index to `nil` will introduce a hole in the array. These holes can sometimes cause unexpected issues.

The size of an array

Just as you are able to find the length of a string with the # operator, you can find the length of an array as well. This is because the # operator gives back the size of a table. We can use this operator to loop through an array that has a dynamic size, for example, such as the following code snippet:

```
arr = { "a", "b", "c", "d", "e", "f", "g" }

length = #arr
print ("array length: " .. length)

for i=1,#arr do
  print (arr[i])
end
```

The length operator # will only count array elements starting from index 1. This means if you use index 0, it will not be counted towards the number of elements in the array:

```
arr = { }

arr[0] = "x" -- not counted towards length
arr[1] = "y"
arr[2] = "z"

length = #arr -- length = 2!
print ("array length: " .. length)
```

Trying to find the length of a sparse array is tricky. The # considers an array over if it finds two nil values one after the other. For example, in this code, the length of the array is incorrectly reported as 2:

```
arr = { }

arr[1] = "x"
arr[2] = "y"
-- Skipping 3 & 4, at least 2 nils after each other end the array
arr[5] = "z" -- not counted towards length
arr[6] = "w" -- not counted towards length

length = #arr -- length = 2, which is WRONG!
print ("array length: " .. length)
```

Because of this unintuitive behavior, using the # operator to find the length of an array is considered to be unreliable. A better way of finding the length of an array will be covered later in this chapter, in the *Iterating* section.

The behavior of the length operator is documented in the Lua 5.2 manual under section *3.4.6 - The Length Operator*, found online at https://www.lua.org/manual/5.2/manual.html.

Multidimensional arrays

Some languages such as C# have native support for multidimensional arrays; Lua does not. You can create a multidimensional array in Lua by creating an array of arrays (really a table of tables). Doing so means you have to declare every element of an array to be a new row in the matrix or another array. You can achieve this as follows:

```
num_rows = 4
num_cols = 4

matrix = {} -- create new matrix
for i=1,num_rows do
  matrix[i] = {} -- create new row
  for j=1,num_cols do
    matrix[i][j] = i * j -- Assign value to row i, column j
  end
end
```

Once you have a matrix with several rows created, you can use double brackets to access elements within the matrix. The following piece of code shows this:

```
num_rows = 4
num_cols = 4

values = { 'A', 'B', 'C', 'D',
           'E', 'F', 'G', 'H',
           'I', 'J', 'K', 'L',
           'M', 'N', 'O', 'P'}
value = 1

matrix = {} -- create new matrix

for i=1,num_rows do
  matrix[i] = {} -- create new row

  for j=1,num_cols do
    -- current element: row i, column j
    -- assign current value to element
    matrix[i][j] = values[value] -- assign element to column
```

```
      value = value + 1 -- move to next letter
   end
end

-- print some elements
print (matrix[1][1])
print (matrix[2][4])
print (matrix[3][4])
```

Iterating

In Lua, you can iterate over all elements of a table or an array using the generic for loop. The generic for is similar to the numeric for loop discussed in the last chapter, but with subtle differences in syntax.

The generic for loop consists of the `for` keyword followed by a variable list, followed by the `in` keyword, followed by an expression list, and finally a `do-end` chunk. The code looks like the following:

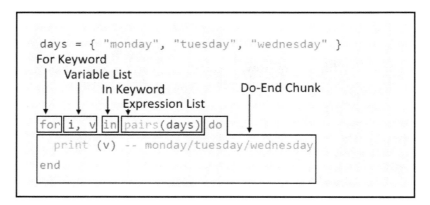

The first variable in the variable list is the control variable. On each iteration, the for loop evaluates the expressions in the list and assigns their results to the variable list. The loop keeps executing while the control variable is not `nil`.

The expression list of a for loop usually consists of a single iterator function. Lua provides several built-in iterators for different tasks. This section will explore how the `pairs` iterator, which has a key and a value, is used to iterate a table and how the `ipairs` iterator, which has an index and a value, is used to iterate an array.

Understanding pairs

The `pairs` iterator function is provided by Lua; it is used to iterate over a table. The pairs function returns two variables—let's call them `k` and `v`. The `k` variable will contain the key being iterated over and the `v` variable will contain the value. `v` can be `nil`, but `k` cannot. The following code demonstrates using pairs to iterate over a simple table:

```
vector = { x = 34, y = 22, z = 56 }

for k, v in pairs(vector) do
  print ("key: " .. k .. ", value: " .. v)
end
```

Understanding ipairs

The `ipairs` iterator is used to iterate over arrays. `ipairs` returns two variables—let's call them `i` and `v`. The `i` variable will hold the index of the element being iterated over, `v` will hold the value of the element. The following code demonstrates using `ipairs` to iterate over an array:

```
days = { "monday", "tuesday", "wednesday", "thursday", "friday",
"saturday", "sunday" }

for i, v in ipairs(days) do
  print ("index: " .. i .. ", value: " .. v)
end
```

Closures

Closures capture the enclosing state of a chunk. A great example of this is having a function that returns an anonymous function. The anonymous function can see the local variables of the enclosing function. However, because the anonymous function is returned, it can outlive the existing function.

When returning an anonymous function, it creates a closure. This closure captures its enclosing state (visible chunks). This mechanism lets you access the state of the enclosing function, even though that function is no longer executing. This description may sound confusing, but the code for it is pretty straightforward:

```
function NextNumber()
  -- local to the NextNumber function
  local currentNumber = 0
```

```
      return function () -- anonymous function
        -- Because this anonymous function is
        -- created inside the NextNumber function
        -- it can see all members of NextNumber
        -- this function will remember the state
        -- of NextNumber, creating a closure!

        currentNumber = currentNumber + 1

        return currentNumber
    end
end

-- Assign the anonymous function to the variable next
next = NextNumber()
-- At this point, NextNumber has finished executing.

print (next()) -- call anonymous function using next
print (next()) -- call anonymous function using next
print (next()) -- call anonymous function using next

-- currentNumber does not exist in a global context!
print (currentNumber) -- will print nil
```

The `NextNumber` function in this example is often called a factory. The function is called a factory because every time you call the function, it produces a new closure. You can then call the resulting function.

Iterator functions

Closures can be used to create a custom iterator. In this section, you will build a custom iterator that will walk through an array, returning only the value stored in each index, not the index itself. The first time the iterator encounters a `nil` variable, it will terminate. This custom iterator will work with the generic for loop. A generic for loop holds on to three variables:

- The iterator function, this is your closure
- An invariant state
- A control variable, the first variable returned by the iterator function

When a generic for executes, it evaluates the expressions after the in keyword. These expressions should result in the three values kept by the for: the iterator function, the invariant state, and the initial value for the control variable. If only one item is returned (in this case, an iterator function), the other two variables get `nil` values:

```
days = { "monday", "tuesday", "wednesday", "thursday" }

function walk(array)
  local index = 0

  return function()
    index = index + 1

    return array[index]
  end
end

for day in walk(days) do
  print (day)
end
```

The `walk` function in this code is the iterator factory. It takes an array and returns a closure. This closure returns every sequential index of the array argument. Once a `nil` value is returned, the generic for loop stops executing. The `array` argument and `index` variable in this code are both local to the `walk` function. This means once you execute the initial `walk` function, the local variables of that function are only accessible to the closure created by the function.

Meta tables

In Lua, meta tables can be used to modify the behavior of tables. Any table can be made into a meta table, and any table can have a meta table. Even meta tables can have their own meta tables. Meta tables change the behavior of tables using meta methods. These meta methods are functions with a specific name that affect how a table behaves.

First, create a table named meta. For now, this is a normal table. This table will have a function named __add. __add is a reserved function name. The __add function will take two arguments.

The left argument will be a table with a field called `value`, the right argument will be a number:

```
meta = { } -- Creates table
meta.__add = function(left, right) -- adds meta method
    return left.value + right -- left is assumed to be a table.
end
```

Next, make a table called container. The container table will have a variable called value, with a value of 5:

```
container = {
  value = 5
}
```

Try to add the number 4 to the container table; Lua will throw a syntax error. This is because you can't add a number to a table. The code that causes the error looks like the following:

```
result = container + 4 -- ERROR
print ("result: " .. result)
```

By adding a meta table to the container table, which has an __add meta method, we can make this code work. The `setmetatable` function is used to assign a meta table. The code to make this all work looks like this:

```
setmetatable(container, meta) -- Set meta table
result = container + 4 -- Works!
print ("result: " .. result)
```

When Lua tries to add anything to a table, it checks whether the table has a meta table. If the table does have a meta table, and that meta table has an __add meta method, it is executed for the addition. This means the following line of code:

```
result = container + 4
```

Is actually executed as:

```
result = meta.__add(container, 4)
```

Meta tables are perhaps the most powerful feature of Lua; however ,this concept can quickly become confusing. You can read more about meta tables at the following website: `http://lua-users.org/wiki/MetamethodsTutorial`.

setmetatable

When you create a new table, Lua does not give it a meta table. That is, by default a table will have a `nil` value for its meta table. You can assign a meta table to a table using the `setmetatable` method. This method takes two arguments, both are tables. The first argument is the target table, the second argument is the new meta table.

You can of course set any table to be a meta table of any other table. You can even self-assign a meta table, like the following:

```
container = {
  value = 5,
  __add = function(l, r)
    return l.value + r.value
  end
}

setmetatable(container, container)
result = container + container
print ("result: " .. result)
```

In this example, the container table has an __add method. Setting the container table to be its own meta table makes the following statement:

```
result = container + container
```

Execute as if it were actually written like this:

```
result = container.__add(container.value, container.value)
```

getmetatable

Complementary to the `setmetatable` method, you can retrieve the meta table of a table using the `getmetatable` method. `getmetatable` takes only one argument, a table. If the table provided has a meta table, the meta table will be returned, otherwise `getmetatable` will return `nil`:

```
x = {}
y = {}
z = {}

setmetatable(y, z)

print (getmetatable(x))
print (getmetatable(y))
```

This will print `nil` for x, as it has no meta table, and some large, random number for y. This large, random-looking number is the unique ID for table z.

__index

When you try to access a nonexistent field in a table, the result is `nil`. However, if the table being accessed has a meta table and that meta table has an __index meta method, the meta method will be called.

There are two tables, x and y. Neither table has a `hello` key, but both tables try to print this key. In both instances, the print statement will result in `nil`:

```
x = {
   foo = "bar"
}
y = { }

print (x.foo) -- bar
print (x.hello) -- nil

print (y.foo) -- nil
print (y.hello) -- nil
```

To fix this, create a meta table with an __index meta method. _index takes two arguments. The first argument is the table that is being indexed, the second argument is the key.

The following code creates two meta tables, z and w; both have an __index meta method. Table z uses this meta method to return a variable found in itself, while w manually checks the key and returns some inline string. Table x is assigned the z meta method, table y is assigned the w meta method:

```lua
x = {
  foo = "bar"
}

y = { }

z = {
  hello = "world z",
  __index = function(table, key)
    return z[key]
  end
}

w = {
  __index = function(table, key)
    if key == "hello" then
      return "inline world"
    end
    return nil
  end
}

setmetatable(x, z)
setmetatable(y, w)

print (x.foo) -- bar
print (x.hello) -- world z

print (y.foo) -- nil
print (y.hello) -- inline world
```

In this code, when printing x.foo, the foo field of the x table is printed. When printing x.hello, Lua sees that table x does not have a hello field, but it does have a meta table and that meta table has an __index function. Lua then passes table x and hello as the arguments to the __index function of the meta table, which returns the hello field of table z.

When printing y.foo, Lua sees that table y does not have a hello field, but it does have a meta table with an __index meta method. The __index meta method of table w is called, with table y and foo as arguments. This meta method only returns a value if the key provided is hello. Since the key provided is not hello, the __index meta method returns nil.

__newindex

The __newindex meta method is complementary to the __index meta method. Where __index is used to retrieve values from missing keys in a table, __newindex is used to assign values to missing keys. The __newindex method takes three arguments:

- The table that is being operated on
- The missing key
- The value being assigned

Here is an example of using the __newindex meta method:

```
x = { }
y = { }

z = {
  __index = function(table, key)
    return z[key]
  end,
  __newindex = function(table, key, value)
    z[key] = value
  end
}

setmetatable(x, z)
setmetatable(y, z)

x.foo = "bar"

print (x.foo)
print (y.foo)
print (z.foo)
```

In this example, both tables x and y have meta table z. The z meta table has an __index meta method, which searches for a key within z whenever a nonexistent key is accessed. It also has a __newindex meta method, which sets a new key value pair in the z meta table if x or y don't have the key present already.

When executing the line x.foo = "bar", Lua sees that x does not have a foo member, but it does have a meta table with the __newindex meta method present. Lua then calls the __newindex meta method of the meta table (z), which assigns the key value pair to table z.

When printing the foo key of either table x or y, the __index meta method of their meta table, z, is invoked, returning the foo value stored in z.

rawget and rawset

Even if a table has an __index or __newindex meta method, values in that table can still be set directly. These meta methods can be bypassed with the rawset and rawget functions, which set and get the values of a table directly.

rawget takes two arguments, the table being accessed and the key being retrieved. It has the following signature:

```
rawget(table, key)
```

rawset takes three arguments, the table being accessed, the key being set, and the value being set. It has the following signature:

```
rawset(table, key, value)
```

To demonstrate how this works, let's use the previous sample code to set the foo member of table x directly:

```
x = { }
y = { }

z = {
  __index = function(table, key)
    return z[key]
  end,
  __newindex = function(table, key, value)
    z[key] = value
  end
}

setmetatable(x, z)
setmetatable(y, z)

x.foo = "bar" -- Sets "bar" in z
rawset(x, "foo", "raw") -- Sets "raw" in x directly!
```

```
print (x.foo) -- raw, lives in x
print (y.foo) -- bar, lives in z
```

__call

The __call meta method lets a table be used as a function. In some languages, this construct is referred to as a functor; in Lua it's called a **functable**.

The __call meta method has a variable number of arguments. The first argument is the table being treated as a function; this is followed by any number of arguments that the functable actually takes. Let's see this in action:

```
tbl = {
  __call = function(table, val1, val2)
    return "Hello, from functor: " .. (val1 + val2)
  end
}

setmetatable(tbl, tbl)
message = tbl(2, 3); -- Calling the table like a function!
print ("message: " .. message)
```

You can pass less arguments to the functable; any arguments not present will simply receive a nil value. You can also pass more arguments to the functable; additional arguments are simply dropped. Functables are an easy way to couple state with a function.

Operators

Lua also provides meta methods for a number of operators, such as addition or subtraction. Often, these meta methods might be performed on two separate tables. The rules for which tables a meta method is executed on are as follows:

- If the left-hand side of the expression has a meta method, but the right-hand side doesn't, the meta method of the left-hand side is used
- If the right-hand side of the expression has a meta method, but the left-hand side doesn't, the meta method of the right-hand side is used
- If both sides of the expression have meta methods, the meta method of the left-hand side is used

Math operators

All of the following are binary mathematical operators. The meta method for each of these operators takes two arguments, the left- and the right-hand side of the equation. Each of the functions takes the following general form:

```
meta = {
  __<method> = function(left, right)
    -- Do stuff
  end
}
```

Here are the names and a brief description of each binary mathematical meta method:

- __add: **Addition**, when writing "table + object" or "object + table"
- __sub: **Subtraction**, when writing "table - object" or "object - table"
- __mul: **Multiplication**, when writing "table * object" or "object * table"
- __div: **Division**, when writing "table / object" or "object / table"
- __mod: **Modulo**, when writing "table % object" or "object % table"
- __pow: **Involution**, when writing "table ^ object" or "object ^ table"

Equivalence operators

There are three meta methods used to compare objects for equality. For these meta methods to work, both tables must have the same comparison meta method! Each of these meta methods takes two arguments, the tables being compared:

- __eq: Check for equality, when `table1 == table2` is evaluated
- _lt: Check for less than, when `table1 < table2` is evaluated
- __le: Check for less than or equal to, when `table1 <= table2` is evaluated

The __eq meta method checks equality; for example, the expression `table1 == table2` is actually evaluated as `getmetatable(table1).__eq(table1, table2)`. But, this _eq meta method is also used to check for inequality. The expression `table1 ~= table2` is evaluated as `not (a == b)`, which can be expanded into `not getmetatable(table1).__eq(table1, table2)`.

The __lt operator checks whether one argument is less than the other one. The __lt meta method is also used to check for greater than by simply swapping the arguments when the expression is evaluated. The less than or equal to operator also uses the same logic to check for greater than or equal to tests.

Other operators

There are a few miscellaneous meta methods that might be useful. These misc meta methods are mainly focused around string-like operations:

- __tostring: Expected to return a string representation of a table. Takes a single argument, the table being converted to a string.
- __len: Expected to return the length of the table when writing #table. Takes a single argument, the table whose length we are trying to find.
- __concat: Expected to concatenate two tables when writing table1 .. table2. This function does not have to return a string, but for the sake of consistency it probably should. This function takes two arguments, the tables being concatenated.

Objects

Many programming languages support the concept of **Object-Oriented Programming** (**OOP**). OOP is a methodology that couples data (variables) and logic (functions) into one cohesive unit (object). While Lua is not an object-oriented language, it does provide all the facilities to allow us to implement an object system.

The class is a core construct in OOP. The class is a single template from which multiple objects can be built. A common analogy is to compare a class to the blueprint of a house. The blueprint defines the dimensions and layout of a house, and many houses can be produced from a single blueprint.

Even though many houses can be made from the same blueprint, they are independent of each other. If one home owner adds a room to a house, it will not affect any other houses. But, if a room is added to the blueprint of that house, all future houses will have that room.

Some languages, such as C++ and Java, provide native support for classes, but Lua does not. Instead, in Lua a clever use of meta tables can create a class system. Meta tables can create a prototype-based object system similar to what is found in JavaScript or Action Script.

Classes

A class is the template or blueprint that object instances are built from. A class defines variables and functions that every object made from that class is guaranteed to have. Each object, however, has its own copy of these variables, independent of each other.

For example, if we have a class to represent the enemies in a game, we can assume that each enemy has some health, an attack value, and some defense value. This is pretty easy to code up:

```
Enemy = {  }
Enemy.health = 200
Enemy.attack = 4
Enemy.defense = 20
```

This `Enemy` table will serve as the blueprint for all enemy objects. So, how can you create new objects from this blueprint? In OOP terms, a constructor is needed. A constructor is a function that instantiates a new object from a class. In Lua, this constructor is just a function that does some special things; by convention, this function is usually called `new`. For the enemy class, it's going to be `Enemy.new`.

The constructor for the enemy object will need to take two arguments. The first argument is the actual `Enemy` table; the constructor needs to know that this is the class being used to instantiate the new object. The second argument is an optional table, which represents the object to create. If no table is provided, a new table (object) will be created.

The constructor needs to assign the object instance's meta table to be the `Enemy` table. Once the meta table is set, assign the __index meta method to be the same as the __index meta method of the `Enemy` table:

```
-- By convention, the first argument should be names self.
-- The reason for this will be explained later in this section
Enemy.new = function (self, object)
    object = object or {} -- Use provided table, or create new one
    setmetatable(object, self) -- Assign meta table
    self.__index = self
    return object
end
```

This code sets the new object's meta table to be the `Enemy` table. After the meta table is set, the __index meta method of the object to be the Enemy table as well. Whenever a field is accessed on the new object, if that field does not exist, it will return the Enemy table's copy of that field.

The constructor, `Enemy.new`, can be called like any other function. The first argument is mandatory, but the second argument is optional. The following code creates three objects from the `Enemy` class. Two of the three objects have unique health values:

```
grunt = Enemy.new(Enemy) -- Health is stored in "Enemy"
miniBoss = Enemy.new(Enemy) -- Health is stored in "Enemy"
boss = Enemy.new(Enemy, { health = 500, defense = 100 } ) -- Health is
stored in "boss"

miniBoss.health = 250 -- Health is now stored in "miniBoss"

-- grunt does not have a health variable, so the enemy table health is
returned
print ("grunt health: " .. grunt.health)
-- miniBoss has a health variable, it was created in the above assignment
print ("mini boss health: " .. miniBoss.health)
-- boss also has a health variable, so the boss table health is returned
print ("boss health: " .. boss.health)
```

Objects, by definition, combine state and logic. So far, the `Enemy` class only contains state. The following code adds a `hit` function to the `Enemy` class. This function would be called whenever the player hits an enemy, causing damage. As such, the function will take two arguments. The first argument is the table that represents the enemy being attacked (in this case, `grunt` or `boss`) and the second argument is how much damage is being done:

```
-- By convention, the first argument should be names self
-- The reason for this will be explained later in this section
Enemy.hit = function(self, damage)
    damage = damage - self.defense
    if damage < 0 then
        damage = 0
    end
    self.health = self.health - damage
end
```

Even though the `hit` function is a field inside the `Enemy` table, we never reference `Enemy.health` directly. Instead, we use the first argument of the function, `self`, to determine which enemy to attack. This is because the `Enemy` table is a class not an instance. The Enemy instances are `grunt` or `boss`. The first argument to this function is expected to be an enemy instance.

The following code snippet shows how we can use the new `hit` function. Because the function belongs to the `Enemy` table, we call `Enemy.hit`. Unlike the constructor, the first argument to the function is an instance of the `Enemy` table not the table itself:

```
print ("Hero attacks both boss and grunt")

Enemy.hit(boss, 50)
Enemy.hit(grunt, 55)

print ("grunt health: " .. grunt.health)
print ("boss health: " .. boss.health)
```

The enemy table only set its __index meta method not the __newindex meta method. This means before the hit function executes, `grunt.health` actually returns the health field stored in the `Enemy` table. But the hit function contains the following piece of code:

```
self.health = self.health - damage
```

When the function is called `self` is a reference to `grunt`, a new field named `health` is added to `grunt`. After that line of code executes, `grunt` will have its own `health` field and no longer return `Enemy.health`. This all works because the __index meta method is set, but the __newindex meta method is not.

While the code presented in this section has been object-oriented, the syntax has not. Lua actually provides some syntax sugar for working with objects. The next section talks about Lua's syntactic sugar for OOP programming and the `self` argument.

The : operator

In the previous section, you implemented some object-oriented principles by building an enemy class, instantiating several enemies and calling some methods on the enemy instances. While all of the code was technically correct, each enemy instance had to be passed to the function stored in the enemy class.

Lua provides some syntactic sugar for calling functions on objects, the colon (`:`) operator.

This operator automatically provides the first argument to a function. This first argument, by convention, is called `self`. You can call this first argument whatever you want, but following convention will make your code easy to read and maintain.

The following bit of code demonstrates how the colon operator is used in comparison to the dot operator:

```
Vector = {
  x = 0,
  y = 1,
  z = 0
}

Vector.new = function (self, object)
    object = object or {} -- Use provided table, or create new one
    setmetatable(object, self) -- Assign meta table
    self.__index = self
    return object
end

Vector.print = function(self)
    print("x:" .. self.x .. ", y: " .. self.y .. ", z: " .. self.z)
end

-- same as Vector.new(Vector, nil)
velocity = Vector:new()

-- Same as Vector.new(Vector, {x=20,z=10})
momentum = Vector:new({x = 20, z = 10})

-- Using the dot syntax, the print method of the
-- Vector class is called, and the object instance
-- is passed as it's first variable (self)
Vector.print(velocity)
Vector.print(momentum)

-- Using the colon syntax, the print method can be
-- called on instances of the Vector class. The colon
-- operator will fill in the first variable (self), with
-- the object instance it is being called on
velocity:print()
momentum:print()
```

The colon syntax makes calling the function more convenient. Remember, before this operator, each function had to be called on the Enemy table with the first argument being the Enemy table, like the following:

```
grunt = Enemy.new(Enemy)
boss = Enemy.new(Enemy, { health = 500, defense = 100 } )
```

Using the colon syntax, that is no longer needed. Because the Enemy table is on the left-hand side of the colon, it will automatically be provided as the first variable, in this case named `self`. The previous code could be rewritten as follows:

```
grunt = Enemy:new()  -- self = Enemy
boss = Enemy:new({ health = 500, defense = 100 } )  -- self = Enemy
```

Using the colon operator makes calling member functions simpler as well. Before using the colon operator, the `hit` function had to be called on the `Enemy` class, with the first argument being the instance of the class to affect:

```
Enemy.hit(boss, 50)
Enemy.hit(grunt, 55)
```

The colon operator provides whatever is on its left side as the first argument to the function being called. This makes it possible to call methods on objects instead of the class:

```
boss:hit(50)
grunt:hit(55)
```

This code works because `boss:hit(50)` is just syntactic sugar for `Enemy.hit(boss, 50)`. How does Lua know that the `Enemy` table has a `hit` function, not the `boss` table? Because the `boss` table's `__index` meta method points at `Enemy`. When Lua sees that `boss.hit(boss, 50)` is invalid but boss has an `__index` meta method, it tries to call the function using the meta method.

Tables inside of objects

The object system described only works if a class contains values; it falls apart when the class contains a reference (like a table). This happens because tables are passed by reference not value. When the `__index` meta function returns a table contained in a class, there is no new copy of that table, just a reference that is shared among every instance of the class. The following code demonstrates this:

```
Character = {
    alive = true
}

Character.position = {
  x = 10, y = 20, z = 30
}

Character.new = function(self, object)
  object = object or {}
```

```
    setmetatable(object, self)
    self.__index = self
    return object
end

player1 = Character:new()
player2 = Character:new()

player1.position.x = 0
player2.position.y = 10

print ("Player 1, position: ("
.. player1.position.x .. ", " .. player1.position.y
.. ", " .. player1.position.z .. ")")

print ("Player 2, position: ("
.. player2.position.x .. ", " .. player2.position.y
.. ", " .. player2.position.z .. ")")

if player1.position == player2.positon then
  print ("Player 1 and 2 have the same position reference");
else
  print ("Player 1 and 2 have unique positon tables");
end

print ("Table id:")
print ("Player 1: " .. tostring(player1.position))
print ("Player 2 :" .. tostring(player2.position))
```

This can be fixed by making sure that each instance of the `Character` class has a unique copy of the position table. The best place to add this table is in the constructor, before the `__index` meta method is assigned. That is, the `new` function must assign per instance member tables before setting the meta table of an object. This code fixes the problem with the previous code sample:

```
Character.new = function(self, object)
  object = object or {}

  -- Assign per instance variables after the object is valid
  -- but before setting the meta table! Copy all members of
  -- the new table by value!
  object.position = {}
  object.position.x = Character.position.x
  object.position.y = Character.position.y
  object.position.z = Character.position.z

  setmetatable(object, self)
```

```
    self.__index = self
    return object
end
```

Inheritance

A key concept in OOP is inheritance. Inheritance allows one class to inherit functionality from another class. The class being inherited from is the parent class, the class that inherits is the child class. Another way to say this is that the child class derives from the parent class.

The child class can access all the variables and functions of its parent class. In addition to access, the child class can provide its own implementation for any function inherited from the parent class. The child class re-implementing a function of a parent class is known as function overriding.

Inheritance does not have to be linear. Single inheritance allows one object to inherit functionality from only one direct ancestor. Multiple inheritance allows one child class to have multiple parent classes.

Multiple inheritance has some inherent problems. One of the biggest problems of multiple inheritance is the diamond problem. The diamond problem involves having two base classes, let's say class A and class B. Both classes implement a function named foo. When the child class tries to access foo, should it access the inherited function from class A or from class B?

Single inheritance

When using single inheritance, any class can inherit functionality from only one super class. To implement single inheritance, create a new class through an existing constructor. This can be a bit confusing, so let's see an example.

Start by creating an `Animal` class; this will be the base class:

```
Animal = {
    sound = ""
}

Animal.new = function(self, object)
    object = object or {}
    setmetatable(object, self)
    self.__index = self
```

```
        return object
    end

    Animal.MakeSound = function(self)
        print(self.sound)
    end
```

Not every animal is going to make the same sound. Create two new classes, dog and cat, that extend Animal:

```
    -- Dog is a class, not an object (instance)
    Dog = Animal:new()
    Dog.sound = "woof"
    -- Cat is a class, not an Object (instance)
    Cat = Animal:new()
    Cat.sound = "meow"
    Cat.angry = false
    Cat.MakeSound = function(self)
        if self.angry then
            print("hissss)
        else
            print(self.sound)
        end
    end
```

In this code, Dog is a new class, not an instance of the Animal class. This can be a bit tricky at first, as the syntax is similar. Dog simply overrides the sound variable. Cat also extends Animal. But Cat provides its own implementation of MakeSound, which lets the cat make different sounds.

Regardless of whether an animal is a Cat or a Dog, we can treat them both as an Animal. We know that every object that is a Cat or a Dog is also an Animal. And we know that every Animal has a MakeSound function. The following code generates some animals and has them all make sounds:

```
    animals = { Cat:new(), Dog:new(), Cat:new() }
    animals[1].angry = true

    for i,v in ipairs(animals) do
        -- The current animal is stored in the v variable.
        -- It doesn't matter if the animal is a Dog or a Cat
        -- Both Dog and Cat extend Animal, which is guaranteed to contain a
    MakeSound function.
        v:MakeSound()
    end
```

Multiple inheritance

Multiple inheritance gets messy; languages such as Java and C# don't actually support it. Multiple inheritance also tends to lead to deep, complicated class hierarchies. These complex hierarchies make multiple inheritance hard to debug. The rest of this book will use single inheritance, avoiding the intricacies of multiple inheritance.

> Interested in implementing multiple inheritance? An implementation guide can be found online at `https://www.lua.org/pil/16.3.html`.

Summary

In this chapter, you learned how to use tables. Tables are the only data structure available in Lua; they are Lua's most powerful feature. We looked at how to implement a fully working object system using tables. This kind of extension to the language itself is what makes Lua so powerful.

4
Lua Libraries

In Chapter 3, *Tables and Objects*, you learned how to use one of Lua's most powerful features: tables. This chapter will build on that knowledge by introducing the global table, some of Lua's built-in modules, and how to create custom modules. By the end of this chapter, you should be able to put classes into modules to make them as reusable as possible.

In this chapter, we will cover the following topics:

- The global table
- The Lua math library
- The Lua file IO library
- Interfacing with the operating system
- More strings
- Creating and loading modules

Technical requirements

You will be required to have JavaScript programming language. Finally, to use the Git repository of this book, the user needs to install Git.

The code files of this chapter can be found on GitHub:
https://github.com/PacktPublishing/Lua-Quick-Start-Guide/tree/master/Chapter04

Check out the following video to see the code in action:
http://bit.ly/2v5rObE

The global table

The one thing you really need to understand about Lua is that just about everything in it is a table. Global variables in Lua (variables not declared local) live in an invisible, global table. This table is exposed as _G. This global table is just like any other table in Lua; you can perform the exact same operations on it. This section will explore two methods of working with the functionality of the global table.

Explicit variables

The loose, typed nature of variables in Lua can be great for prototyping games quickly, but it can also lead to a lot of bugs! For example, consider the following code:

```
five21 = 521 -- Variable name ends with a 1

for i=1,1000 do
  if i == five21 then
    five2l = "Five Twenty One" -- ERROR! Variable name ends with an l
    break
  end
end

print("value: " .. five21)
```

Can you spot the problem? During the first assignment, the five21 variable ends with a 1, but in the second assignment it ends with a lower case l. Characters such as 0 and O, 1 and l, or I and l can lead to easy typos depending on the font being used.

You can fix these types of typos using explicit variable declaration. Set the __newindex and __index metamethods of the global table to track whether a variable being used has been declared or not. This implies that you will need to create a function to declare variables, and a table to track all declared variables.

This is a bit unintuitive, but it's another example of how powerful Lua is. First, create the table that will store a list of variables that have been declared, and set the meta table for _G:

```
_G.declared = {}
setmetatable(_G, _G)
```

Next, create the Declare function. This will simply set a flag in the declared table to true:

```
_G.Declare = function(k, v)
    _G.declared[k] = true
end
```

The __index metamethod of _G should only return values if the key being retrieved is present in the declared table. Here, use `rawget` to avoid a recursive call:

```
_G.__index = function(t, k)
    if not _G.declared[k] then
        print ("Can't read undeclared variable: " .. k)
        return nil
    end
    return rawget(t, k)
end
```

Similarly, the __newindex metamethod must first check whether a variable has been declared. If so, this function uses `rawset` to add the new key to the global table:

```
_G.__newindex = function(t, k, v)
    if not _G.declared[k] then
        print ("Can't write undeclared variable: " .. k)
    else
        rawset(t, k, v)
    end
end
```

The following code demonstrates how to use the preceding changes in the global table:

```
Declare("x") -- Declare in _G
Declare("y") -- Declare in _G

x = 21
y = 22

print (x .. ", " .. y)

z = 5 -- Can't add to _G if not declared
print (z)

local w = 19 -- Local to the file, not in _G
print ("w: " .. w)
```

The preceding code declares variables x and y, putting both keys into the declared table. Next, it assigns values to the variables that invoked the _newindex metamethod. Because the variables have been declared, they are allowed to be set, otherwise an error would occur. After that, the print statement invokes the __index metamethod, which retrieves the variables.

When a value is assigned to `z`, the `__newindex` metamethod sees that this variable was not declared and prints a warning. Because the variable is not declared, trying to print the value of `z` also results in an expected error. The `w` variable is created local to the current Lua file; it will not be recorded in the global table `_G`.

Dynamic variables

Because the global table is just a table, it can be indexed dynamically. You can concatenate strings to index the global table using the square bracket notation. For example, the following three lines of code all do the same thing:

```
foo = "bar"
_G.foo = "bar"
_G["foo"] = "bar"
```

In the preceding code example, the last line indexes the global environment with a string. The following code demonstrates how to index the global table using dynamic strings:

```
value1 = 'x'
value2 = 'y'
value3 = 'z'

for i = 1,3 do
    print ("value" .. i .. ": " .. _G["value" .. i])
end
```

Environment

Lua provides an easy and powerful method to set the global environment per function. This means that any variables without the `local` modifier will be recorded in the environment of the function, rather than in the global table. This can be achieved by setting the `_ENV` variable inside a function.

The `_ENV` variable, by default, points to `_G`. This means any new variable will be registered in `_G`. But if you declare `_ENV` to be a new table, for example, variables will be registered to it instead of `_G`:

```
function SayHelloCustomEnv()
    local _ENV = {print=print}

    foo = "hello"
    local bar = "world"
```

```
        print(foo .. " " .. bar)
end

function SayHelloDefaultEnv()
    foo = "hello"
    local bar = "world"

    print(foo .. " " .. bar)
end

-- foo and bar are not in _G
SayHelloCustomEnv1();
print (foo)
print (bar)

-- foo is declared in _G
SayHelloDefaultEnv();
print(foo)
print(bar)
```

In the preceding code, this line is extremely important:

```
local _ENV = {print=print}
```

First, note that _ENV is declared to be `local`! If you don't declare it as such, _ENV for **ALL** functions will be overwritten. You don't want that.

Second, _ENV is not set to an empty table, it's set to `{print=print}`. This is important. Normally, print lives in _G. But, the function will not be able to access _G anymore. This also means that you can replace any global function with a custom one. For example:

```
function MyPrint(str)
    print("printing: " .. str)
end

function SayHelloCustomEnv()
    local _ENV = {print=print}

    foo = "hello"
    local bar = "world"

    print(foo .. " " .. bar)
end
```

```
-- foo and bar are not in _G
SayHelloCustomEnv();
print (foo)
print (bar)
```

math

At some point, you are likely going to need to change some numbers around. Many mathematical functions such as sine or cosine are provided by Lua. To better understand the provided functions, this section will review Lua's math library.

 The official math library documentation is online here: https://www.lua.org/manual/5.2/manual.html#pdf-math

Trigonometry

Some interactive applications such as games rely heavily on trigonometry. Trigonometry is used to figure out the distance between two points, to render a world, and much more. Lua provides the following trig functions. Remember, all of these functions return radians, not degrees:

- `math.acos(v)`: returns the inverse cosine of a number in radians
- `math.asin(v)`: returns the inverse sine of a number in radians
- `math.atan(v)`: returns the inverse tangent of a number in radians; v is assumed to be x / y
- `math.atan(x, y)`: returns the inverse tangent of a number in radians
- `math.cos(v)`: returns the cosine of a number in radians
- `math.sin(v)`: returns the sine of a number in radians
- `math.tan(v)`: returns the tangent of a number in radians

Changing numbers

Sometimes, it's useful to convert numbers, and for this there are four conversion functions. There are functions to convert between degrees and radians, to get the absolute value of an integer, and to round a floating point number to an integer.

- `math.deg(v)` converts a number from radians to degrees
- `math.rad(v)` converts a number from degrees to radians
- `math.abs(v)` returns the absolute value of the provided number
- `math.tointeger(v)`: if v is convertible to an integer, an integer is returned, otherwise `nil`

Comparing numbers

There are three comparison type functions. Two functions return the min and max of a pair of numbers, and the `ult` function treats both arguments as unsigned integers.

- `math.max(x, y)` returns the smaller number of x or y
- `math.min(x, y)` returns the larger number of x or y
- `math.ult(x, y)` returns `true` if x is less than y, where both x and y are treated as unsigned integers

Randomness

Lua provides a pseudo-random number generator. This means a program will generate the same random number on every run, unless the random number is seeded. The random function can be called with the following arguments:

- `math.random()`: with no arguments generates a real number between 0 and 1
- `math.random(max)`: generates integer numbers between 1 and `max`
- `math.random(min, max)`: generates integer numbers between `min` and `max`

When generating a random number, min and max must be integer values. If the numbers provided are not integers, Lua will cast the numbers to be integers by discarding the decimal part.

To get a random sequence of numbers each time an application is run, the random number generator must be seeded. Seeding the random number genreator means it will return pseudo-random numbers, starting with a different number each time.

For this to work, the seed must be unique each time. To get a mostly unique number, use the current time from the operating system. This should result in unique random numbers each time an application is run:

- `math.randomseed(v)`: seeds random with the value of v
- `os.time()`: returns the number of seconds since *epoch*

Random only needs to be seeded once, at the beginning of the application. The following code implements a simple number-guessing game:

```
math.randomseed(os.time())

print ("Guess a number between 10 and 100!")
number = math.random(10, 100)
-- print ("Random: " .. number)

repeat
    local guess = tonumber( io.read() )
    if guess ~= nil then
        if guess == number then
            print ("You guessed the number.")
            break
        elseif guess < number then
            print ("Too low, guess again.")
        else
            print ("Too high, guess again.")
        end
    end
until false
```

Constants

Lua provides some standard constants. These constants include of the value for **PI (positive infinity)**, the largest number an integer can hold, and the smallest number an integer can hold:

- `math.pi`: the value of pi
- `math.huge`: represents positive infinity

- `math.mininteger`: represents the smallest integer (non-decimal) number
- `math.maxinteger`: represents the largest integer (non-decimal) number

Everything else

There are a number of useful math-related functions Lua offers that do not fit into any of the preceding categories. These functions are listed here, in no particular order:

- `math.ceil(v)`: rounds v up to the nearest integer
- `math.floor(v)`: rounds v down to the nearest integer
- `math.fmod(x, y)`: returns the remainder of the division x / y
- `math.modf(v)`: returns two values, the integer part of v and the factoral part of v
- `math.sqrt(v)`: returns the square root of v
- `math.type(variable)`: returns the strings `integer`, `float`, or `nil`

File IO

At some point, programs will need to work with persistent data. This section explores writing and reading data to and from the hard drive. Lua provides facilities to read and write files through its `io` library. A file doesn't have to contain textual data; you can store data as a binary representation. Reading and writing binary data with Lua is also possible.

Opening a file

When writing to a file or reading from a file, that file needs to be opened first. Lua provides the `io.open` function to open files. On success, the `io.open` function will return a file handle. On failure, it will return `nil`:

```
file = io.open("my_file.txt"); -- Opens existing file in read only mode
```

The preceding line of code will open a file in read-only mode. What if you want to write to a file? The io.open function takes an optional second argument, which is a string. This optional second argument controls the mode in which the file will be opened. Valid values are as follows:

- "r": Read-only mode will let you read the file, but not write to it. This is the default mode for opening the file. If the file does not exist, nil is returned.
- "w": Write mode will create a new file if the specified file name does not exist. If the specified file name exists, it will be overwritten! Allows writing to the file only.
- "a": Append mode opens an existing file, or creates a new one. If the file already exists, its contents remain unchanged and we write data to the end of the file. Allows writing to the file only.
- "r+": Read and write mode for an existing file. This mode will open an existing file and allow us to read from and write to it. If the file already exists, its contents will be overwritten! If the file does not exist, the function returns nil.
- "w+": The same as "w", except this mode allows us to read from the file as well.
- "a+": The same as "a", except this mode allows us to read from the file as well.

If you want to open an existing file for reading and writing, call io.open, like so:

```
file = io.open("my_file.txt", "r+"); -- Opens existing file in read/write
mode
```

The file handle returned by io.open is a Lua object. as such, the colon operator will be used to call methods on this object. The methods of the file handle can read, write, and close the file.

Writing data

Writing data to a file is done with the write function of the file handle. This function will write whatever arguments are passed to it into the file. The following code creates a data.txt file, if one does not exist, or replaces the contents of the existing file:

```
file = io.open("data.txt", "w")
file:write("foo")
file:write("bar")
```

After running the previous code, a `data.txt` file would contain the `foobar` string. Looking at the code, it's reasonable to expect `"foo"` and `"bar"` to be on separate lines. By default, the `write` function does not add any newline characters. You have to add line breaks manually, like so:

```
file = io.open("data.txt", "w")
file:write("foo", "\n")
-- file:write("foo\n") -- would also work
file:write("bar")
```

The `write` function will take any data type as an argument,and will take any number of arguments. The following code demonstrates different ways of concatenating strings being written to a file. The file being written is something you might see being saved as data for a game:

```
-- Create function to save character data
function SaveCharacterData(name, power, team)
  file = io.open("data.txt", "w")
  file:write("name " .. name .. "\n") -- We can concatenate with ..
  file:write("attack ", power, "\n") -- or use a comma seperated list
  file:write("team " .. team, "\n") -- we can even mix & match!
end

-- Call the function
SaveCharacterData("gwen", 20, "blue")
```

Reading data

There are three prominent ways to read a file: either as a huge blob of text, line by line, or one number/string at a time. Reading line by line and one bit of data at a time are relevant to this book.

Reading line by line

The file handle returned by `io.open` has a `lines` member function. This function will return an iterator that can be used to retrieve every line of the file using a loop. The following code demonstrates how to read an entire file, one line at a time:

```
file = io.open("data.txt")
lines = file:lines()
print("Contents of file:");
```

```
for line in lines do
  print("\t" .. line)
end
```

Reading bits of data

The file handle provides a `read` method that can be used to read in only as much data as needed. The `read` method takes one argument, which is a format string, or a number. In case the argument is a number, that number represents how many characters of text to read. The following list contains all of the valid arguments for `read`:

- `"*n"` reads a number; this is the only format that returns a number instead of a string.
- `"*a"` reads the whole file, starting at the current position. At the end of the file, it returns the empty string.
- `"*l"` reads the next line (skipping the end of the line), returning `nil` at the end of the file. This is the default format.
- Providing any *integer number*, (IE: 2) reads a string with up to that number of characters, returning `nil` at the end of the file. If the number is zero, it reads nothing and returns an empty string, or `nil` at the end of the file.

In the code sample for writing data, the `SaveCharacterData` function writes the following text to a file:

```
name gwen
attack 20
team blue
```

To parse this data back into Lua, you will need to call `read` two times for every line. The first read will retrieve and discard the identifier of the line, such as `name` (including the space). The second call to read will read and store our relevant data. The following code demonstrates this:

```
hero = {}
f = io.open("data.txt")

f:read(5) -- read in "name " and discard it
hero.name = f:read() -- Reads to end of line, store name

f:read(7) -- read in "attack " and discard it
hero.health = f:read("*n") -- read the next number

f:read(6) -- read in "team " and discard it
```

```
hero.team = f:read("*l") -- Same as reading in the name

print ("hero")
print ("\tname: " .. hero.name )
print ("\thealth: " .. hero.health)
print ("\tteam: " .. hero.team)
```

Closing a file

Once you are done working with a file, close the file. Not closing the file is considered a resource leak, which can lead to issues until you restart your computer. Closing a file is simple, just call the `close` member function on the file handle. For example:

```
local file = io.open("data.txt", "w")
file:write("foo", "\n")
file:write("bar")
file:close() -- THIS IS NEW! Don't forget to close!
```

Interfacing with the operating system

Lua runs on many operating systems, and as an embedded language can run just about anywhere. The `os` package provides functionality to interface with the underlying operating system in a uniform way.

Working with time

The first function to know when working with time is `os.clock`. This function returns the number of seconds that have elapsed since the Lua program started running. Code tends to run pretty fast, but the following code should print out two different time stamps:

```
print ("Time: " .. os.clock())
for i=1,1000,1 do
  -- Just spin
end
print ("Time: " .. os.clock())
```

Seconds is a very granular measure of time. `os.date` can be used to retrieve less-granular bits of time. This function takes a format string as an argument, and returns the formatted time as a string.

The arguments for os.date are the same as the arguments for the strftime function in C. A full list of arguments is online here: http://www.cplusplus.com/reference/ctime/strftime/

For example, printing out the current time in 24-hour, hour:minute format would be done like so:

```
print ("The time is: " .. os.date("%H:%M"))
```

The os.difftime function will return the difference between two times, provided in seconds. This function can be used to measure how long a piece of code takes to execute. The following example code times a simple loop. The result will likely be 0, as it only takes a few milliseconds to execute a simple loop:

```
local startTime = os.clock()
for i=1,100000,1 do
  -- Do stuff
end
local endTime = os.clock()

local totalTime = os.difftime(startTime, endTime)
print ("The above loop took: " .. totalTime .. " seconds")
```

Interacting with the shell

One of the things that makes Lua powerful as a scripting language is its ability to interact with the operating system through a shell/terminal. os.execute takes a string and returns a status code. Whatever the provided string is will be executed as a shell command. The return value is whatever the running program returned.

If Lua is running embedded in a program, or is on an OS with no shell/terminal, the os.execute command will return 0. You can test if the current Lua environment has a shell by calling os.execute with no arguments. If a non-zero value is returned, a shell is available. If zero is returned, there is no shell or terminal.

The code here tries to pull from git. Using os.execute, Lua could be used to leverage automate a build pipeline:

```
os.execute("git pull")
```

Operating systems have some kind of environment variables. For example, the PATH variable is present on Windows, Linux, and macOS. Lua can access environmental variables using the os.getenv function. The code here prints out the value of the PATH variable:

```
print(os.getenv("PATH"))
```

Working with files

Lua can create, rename, and delete files. We've already seen how to create files in the *File IO* section of this chapter. You can use io.open to create a new file:

```
local file = io.open("new_file.txt", "a")
file:close()
```

Files can be renamed with the os.rename function. This function takes two arguments: the path to the file to be renamed and the path to the final, renamed version of the file. The code here renames the file created in the last sample:

```
os.rename("new_file.txt", "renamed_file.txt")
```

Files can be deleted with the os.remove function. This function takes the path of a file to delete. To remove the previously renamed file, you would have to use the following code:

```
os.remove("renamed_file.txt")
```

Lua can not natively create, rename, enumerate or delete folders, like it can files. All of these functions, however, do exist in each operating system. Lua can use os.execute to perform these actions. For example, you could make a directory on any platform, like so:

```
os.execute("mkdir new_folder")
```

More strings

Chapter 2, *Working With Lua* provided several methods to work with strings. All of these methods where a part of Lua's string library. This section is going to discuss some additional, more advanced methods to deal with strings.

Searching for a substring

Sometimes, you may have a large string (such as the contents of a file) and need to find out if it contains a smaller substring. This can be done with the `string.substring` function. This function takes two variables: the large string to search and a smaller string to look for. On success, it returns a number, which is the index at which the substring first appears. On failure, the function returns `nil`:

```
local sentence = "The quick brown fox"
local word = "quick"

local index = string.find(sentence, word)
print ("substring found at index: " .. index)
```

 The second argument is interesting; it doesn't just have to be a string. The second argument to `string.substring` can be a pattern, which results in regex like searching. For more info, check out `http://lua-users.org/wiki/PatternsTutorial`

Extracting a substring

The `string.sub` function takes three arguments: the string, a start index, and a stop index. The stop index is inclusive. This function will return a substring between the two indices passed. The last argument is optional; if an end index is not provided, `string.sub` will just return everything to the end of the string:

```
local sentence = "The quick brown fox"
local word = "quick"

local start = string.find(sentence, word)
start = start + #word + 1

local result = string.sub(sentence, start)
print("Who was quick?")
print ("the " .. result)
```

All of the functions in the string library are implemented with respect to the : operator. This means that the preceding code could be re-written as follows:

```
local sentence = "The quick brown fox"
local word = "quick"

local start = sentence:find(word)
start = start + #word + 1

local result = sentence:sub(start)
print("Who was quick?")
print ("the " .. result)
```

Case manipulation

Lua provides two functions for case manipulation: upper and lower. As you would expect, these functions transform a string to be upper case or lower case. Like all string functions, these functions are written to work using the colon notation. The code here demonstrates how these functions are used:

```
local sentence = "A rose is a Rose is a ROSE"
print (sentence)

print(string.upper(sentence))
print(string.lower(sentence))

-- OR, use : notation
print(sentence:upper())
print(sentence:lower())
```

Creating and loading modules

Modules allow Lua code to be split across multiple files. The codebase of any non-trivial application is going to get large, and having modules allows the code to be organized and keeps it maintainable. When doing OOP, each class can be its own module. Keeping every class in its own file will keep your projects easy to navigate and maintain.

Lua has several ways of creating and loading modules. Only one method is discussed here. Read more about how modules work at http://lua-users.org/wiki/ModulesTutorial

Creating a module

A module is just a normal Lua table; a module file is a Lua file which returns a table. For us, this means returning an anonymous table. We are going to create a new file, `character.lua`, and declare a character class in this file. The definition of the character class is as follows:

```lua
-- It's important that the table retuned be local!
local character = {}

character.health = 20
character.strength = 5
character.name = ""

character.new = function (self, object)
    object = object or {} -- Use provided table, or create new one
    local provided = ""

    if type(object) == "string" then
        provided = object
        object = {}
    end

    setmetatable(object, self) -- Assign meta table
    self.__index = self

    if provided ~= "" then
        object.name = provided
    end

    return object
end

character.attack = function(self, other)
    print (self.name .. " attacks " .. other.name)
    other.health = other.health - self.strength
    if other.health < 1 then
        print ("\t" .. other.name .. " is dead")
    else
        print ("\t" .. other.name .. " has " .. other.health .. " health
left")
    end
end

return character
```

The previous code creates a table local to the file and returns it. This table has five variables; three of them are values and two are functions. This module represents character class, which has a health, a name, and some strength. The `attack` function will decrease the health of whatever character is being attacked, and print out some information.

The constructor is similar to that seen in previous chapters, except it does a type check on the second argument. This allows the constructor to clone a character object, or to provide a name as a constructor argument.

Loading and using modules

You can load Lua modules with the `require` function. The `require` function takes one argument, which is the name of the file being loaded (without the `.lua` extension). The `require` function should return a table that can then be used as any other table.

The `require` function searches for the given file in several specific folder paths. These paths are stored as a string in the global variable, `package.path`. The default path on windows looks like this:

```
?;?.lua;c:\windows\?;/usr/local/lua/?/?.lua
```

This string contains multiple search paths, each separated by a semicolon (`;`). The `?` charter gets replaced by the filename provided to the `require` function. So, for example, if you called `require("character")`, Lua would look for the following files:

- `./character`
- `./character.lua`
- `c:\windows\character.lua`
- `/usr/local/lua/character/character.lua`

If multiple files exist (namely, both `./character.lua` and `C:\windows\character.lua`), only the first one is loaded. If you call `require` on the same file twice, the module is only loaded one time, avoiding duplicate work.

Let's explore how to use the character module created in the last section. First, make a new file, `game.lua`, in the same directory as *character.lua*. This file should contain the following code:

```
-- load the character module into a table named character
Character = require ("character")

-- Create a new hero, which is a charcter
```

```
gwen = Character:new("gwen")
gwen.strength = 10
-- Create a new enemy, also a character
orc = Character:new("orc")

-- Run game logic
gwen:attack(orc)
orc:attack(gwen)
gwen:attack(orc)
```

The preceding code loads the character module from `character.lua` into a table named `Character`. The loaded Character table is a class that can be used to create new objects. The code creates two character objects and runs a simulated turn-based fight.

There are two major advantages to making something like a game character class into a module. First, there is less code in `game.lua` and other files. Second, the `Character` class is now reusable. You can now use the character class in multiple files, or even multiple projects.

Avoiding parsing

Being able to simply load Lua tables is a powerful mechanism. If you format save data as a valid Lua file, it can be loaded back as a module. Using this feature of Lua, you can avoid having to write code that parses a text file.

Let's explore this concept by first saving some data to disk. The following function saves a simple object containing a level, health, and number of lives to a file named `save.lua`:

```
function Save(level, health, lives)
    file = io.open("save.lua", "w")

    file:write("return { \n")
    file:write("\tlevel = ", level, ",", "\n")
    file:write("\thealth = ", health, ",", "\n")
    file:write("\tlives = ", lives, "\n")
    file:write("}")

    file:close()
end

Save(20, 10, 2)
```

Because `save.lua` is a module, you can load the save data with a single call to `require`, like so:

```
gameData = require("save")
print("Loaded:")
print("\tlevel: " .. gameData.level)
print("\thealth: " .. gameData.health)
print("\tlives: " .. gameData.lives)
```

Executing files

The `require` function only loads a file one time. When dealing with modules, this feature is a great way to avoid loading duplicate code. But, when trying to load data, the `require` function will not re-load data. Loading the same Lua file multiple times can be done using the `dofile` function. Both `dofile` and `require` load a file and execute the code within, but with two major differences:

- `dofile`: will re-load a given file every time it is called
- `dofile`: does not search `package.path`; instead, it loads the file name given assuming the path provided is relative to the current file path

Let's modify the previous code sample to save some data, load it, save some new data, and then re-load the data. The code needs to change to this:

```
Save(20, 10, 2)
gameData = dofile("save.lua")
print("Loaded:")
print("\tlevel: " .. gameData.level)
print("\thealth: " .. gameData.health)
print("\tlives: " .. gameData.lives)

Save(10, 10, 5)
gameData = dofile("save.lua")
print("Loaded:")
print("\tlevel: " .. gameData.level)
print("\thealth: " .. gameData.health)
print("\tlives: " .. gameData.lives)
```

Summary

In this chapter, you learned how to use modules in Lua. Some of the built-in modules for working with files, doing math, and interacting with the operating system were covered. Next, creating your own modules was discussed, as well as guidance on different ways to load Lua source files.

5
Debugging Lua

In the last chapter, you learned how to use some of Lua's, built-in modules and how to create your own module. At this point, you know most of the libraries and concepts Lua has to offer. This chapter will help you understand what to do when unintended bugs creep into your code.

Some of the properties that make Lua extremely powerful also make it easy to introduce unintended bugs. Sometimes, even the simplest of bugs can take a significant amount of effort to fix. Lua provides powerful debug libraries that help make these bugs easier to track down and resolve. In addition to debug libraries, a number of great external tools also exist.

In this chapter, we are going to cover the following topics:

- The debug library
- Error-handling in Lua
- Profiling
- Integrated development environments

Technical requirements

You will be required to have JavaScript programming language. Finally, to use the Git repository of this book, the user needs to install Git.

The code files of this chapter can be found on GitHub:
https://github.com/PacktPublishing/Lua-Quick-Start-Guide/tree/master/Chapter05

Check out the following video to see the code in action:
http://bit.ly/2LBB8OU

The debug library

Lua's debug library is not a debugger. Rather, it is all the building blocks needed to implement a debugger. One thing to remember when writing code against the debug library is it's going to be slow. On top of running your existing code, some extra work has to be done to enable debugging. All code related to the debug library is found in the debug table (module).

The debug library provides *hooks* and *introspective* functions. Hooks let you hook into the runtime to trace what's happening with the program. Introspective functions, on the other hand, let you inspect various aspects of the running code. These aspects involve local variables, the scope of chunks, and so on.

Introspective information

Lua provides the debug.getinfo function to inspect the currently running code. This function takes one of two arguments, either a function or an integer. When the argument is an integer, getinfo will look the specified number of steps up the callstack. For example, let's assume you have the following code:

```
function one()
  print ("one")
end

function two()
  one()
  print("two")
end

function three()
  two()
  print("three")

  debug.getinfo(1)
end
```

Providing an argument of 1 will inspect the function calling debug.getinfo, or function three. Providing 2 will go one more function up the callstack, inspecting function two. Or, providing 3 will look even further up the callstack and inspect function one.

The debug.getinfo return value

No matter what the argument, the `debug.getinfo` function will return a table. This table will contain information about the function being inspected. When called with an integer, the return table will contain the following fields/variables:

- `source`: Where the function is defined. This will contain the name of the file that a function is defined in.
- `short_src`: A short textual version of the function, up to 60 characters.
- `linedefined`: The first line of the source file where the function was defined.
- `lastlinedefined`: The last line in the source file where the function was defined.
- `what`: If the function is a `"Lua"` or a `"C"` function, the appropriate string will be returned.
- `name`: Lua's best guess at the name of the function. In Lua, functions can be assigned to multiple variables, so the name really is a guess most of the time.
- `namewhat`: What the name field is: a `"global"` variable, a `"local"` variable, a `"method"`, a `"field"`, or unknown (`""`).
- `nups`: The number of `up` values for the function.
- `activelines`: The number of lines a function contains. White spaces and comments are ignored.
- `func`: The actual function; you can call this.

Filtering the information

The `debug.info` function is pretty slow, and this happens mostly because of all the data it has to collect. To speed up the function enough, there is an optional second argument that will filter out what variables are present in the return table. The second argument is a string, and it can have any of the following variables:

- `"n"`: Filters name and what the name represents (`namewhat`)
- `"f"`: Filters `func`
- `"S"`: Filters source, `short_src`, what, `linedefined`, and `lastlinedefined`
- `"l"`: Filters currentline
- `"L"`: Filters activelines
- `"u"`: Filters `nup`

You can combine multiple filters in the filter string. For example, to get name and what you would do: debug.info(1, "nS")

Local variables

The local variables of any function can be inspected with the debug.getlocal function. This function takes two arguments: first a stack level (the same as debug.getinfo), and then a variable index. Variables are indexed in the order they appear. If either argument is out of range, the debug.getlocal function will return nil. Otherwise, it will return the name and value of the current variable.

For example, the following code prints the local variables of its calling function:

```
function DebugLocals()
  local info = debug.getinfo(2, "n")
  print ("Local variables of: " .. info.name)

  local idx = 1
  while true do
    local name, val = debug.getlocal(2, idx)
    if name == nil then
      break
    end
    print (" " .. name .. " = " .. tostring(val))
    idx = idx + 1
  end
end

function DoSomething(val1, val2)
  local sum = val1 + val2
  local difference = val1 - val2
  local result = sum * difference

  DebugLocals();
  return result;
end

DoSomething(3, 4)
DoSomething(9, 3)
```

Hooks

Lua provides hooks to monitor an application running in real time. An event handler function can be registered to be executed every time an event or hook happens. There are four types of events that can be hooked into:

- `line`: called every time a line of code is executed
- `call`: called every time a new function is called
- `return`: called every time a function returns
- `counter`: called every x number of instructions, where the caller specifies x.

To register for `line`, `call` or `return`, call `debug.sethook` with a handler function and the first letter of the event being hooked into. For example, registering for `call` events would look like this: `debug.sethoof(function, "c")`. The event handler function should take one argument in all cases, except for the `line` event, when it should take two. The first argument will always be a string describing the event. The optional second argument for `line` will be the line number being executed.

 Once a hook has been set, it can be cleared by calling the `debug.sethook` function with no arguments.

Line ("l")

The first type of `debug.sethook` event is the `line` event. This event is going to fire every time a line of code is being executed. If you've ever used a debugger that supports breakpoints, this is the functionality that could be used to implement breakpoints.

To subscribe to the line event, provide the `debug.sethook` function with two arguments, the even handler and the string `"l"`. The handler function needs to take two arguments. The first argument is going to be a string, with the `"line"` value. The second argument is going to be an integer; this is the line number being executed:

```
function VectorLength(x, y, z)
  local dot = x * x + y * y + z * z
  if dot == 0 then
    return nil
  end
  return math.sqrt(dot)
end
```

```
function trace(event, line)
  print("event: " .. event)
  print ("   executing: line " .. line)
end

debug.sethook(trace, "l")

local x = 3
local y = 5
local z = 1
local len = VectorLength(x, y, z)
print ("length: " .. len)
```

Call ("c")

The next events debug.sethook can hook into are function calls. These events fire every time a function is called. The event handler only needs to take one argument, a string. The value of this string will always be "call". To subscribe to function call events, provide debug.sethook with two arguments: the handler function, and the "c" string. Function callback hooks become much more powerful when combined with the info obtained from debug.getinfo. The following code demonstrates this:

```
function PrintV(x, y, z)
  local out = "(" .. x .. ","
  out = out .. ", " .. y
  out = out .. ", " .. z .. ")"
  return out
end

function MagnitudeSq(x, y, z)
  local magSq = x * x + y * y + z * z
  return magSq;
end

function trace(event)
  local info = debug.getinfo(2)
  if info.what == "Lua" then
    print ("event: " .. event)
    print (" function: " .. info.name)
    print (" defined on: " .. info.linedefined)
  end
end

debug.sethook(trace, "c")

local mSq = MagnitudeSq(9, 2, 6)
```

```
print ("Sqr mag: " .. mSq)
PrintV(9,2,6)
```

Return ("r")

The final type of hook is a return hook. Return hooks get executed every time a function returns, that is, when the `return` keyword is encountered. To subscribe to a return event, provide `debug.sethook` with two arguments: the handler function, and the "r" string.

The handler function takes only one argument, a string constant with the "`return`" value. This callback is similar to the function callback:

```
function Normalize(x, y, z)
  local dot = x * x + y * y + z * z
  if dot == 0 then
    return nil
  end
  local len = math.sqrt(dot)
  return {
    x = x / len,
    y = y / len,
    z = z / len
  }
end

function trace(event)
  local info = debug.getinfo(2)
  if info.what == "Lua" then
    print ("event: " .. event)
    print (" function: " .. info.name)
    print (" defined on: " .. info.linedefined)
  end
end

debug.sethook(trace, "r")

local norm = Normalize(9, 2, 6)
```

Setting a counter

So far, the syntax of `debug.sethook` has been the following:

```
debug.sethook(<handler function>, <"l" | "c" | "r">
```

No matter the event, the function always took two arguments.
The `debug.sethook` function has an optional, third argument: `count`. Providing a count will fire a `"count"` event on every time the specified number of instructions have happened.

Multiple hooks

Multiple hooks can be specified by adding a space and another letter to `debug.sethook`. For example, you could subscribe to every possible event, like so:

```
debug.sethook(trace, "l c r", 1)
```

When subscribing to multiple hooks, remember the callback's second argument is `nil`, except for the `line` event. Check for `nil` as appropriate. The following code demonstrates how to do this:

```
function trace(event, line)
  local info = debug.getinfo(2)
  if info.what == "Lua" then
    print ("event: " .. event)
    print (" function: " .. info.name)
    print (" defined on: " .. info.linedefined)
    if line ~= nil then
      print (" called from: " .. line)
    end
  end
end
```

Traceback

Sometimes, you need to know the call stack of the currently executing code. This can be useful for understanding how to recreate a bug, following code flow, or just to better understand how your code works as a whole. At any point, you can get the current call stack with the `debug.traceback` function. To visually see where in the code you are, just pass the result of this function to print, like so:

```
print(debug.traceback())
```

Debugger.lua

Before moving on, let's take a look at an external debugger solution, one not built into Lua. `dbeugger.lua` is one such solution; it is a debugger written in Lua. You should grab a copy of the `debugger.lua` file from `https://github.com/slembcke/debugger.lua`.

To use `debugger.lua`, you first have to include the module in your source file. This is just a standard call to `require`, for example:

```
local debug = require("debugger")
```

The module that was just included is a functable. That is, it can be called as a function. To set a breakpoint, at any point in your code, just write `debug()`. Whenever one of these `debug()` commands is hit, the flow of execution will be given to the debugger. You can use the following console commands to debug:

- `<enter>`: re-run the last command
- c: **c**ontinue execution
- s: **s**tep forward by one line (into functions)
- n: step forward to the **n**ext line (skipping over functions)
- p: execute the expression and **p**rint the result
- f: step **f**orward until exiting the current function
- u: move **u**p the stack by one frame
- d: move **d**own the stack by one frame
- t: print the stack **t**race
- l: print the function arguments, **l**ocals, and upvalues
- q: **q**uit the program

Using debugger.lua

Lets take a look at an example of using `debugger.lua`. Consider the following buggy code:

```
local debug = require("debugger")

function BuggyAdditionFunction(x1, x2)
  local sum = x1 * x2
  debug()
  return sum
end
```

```
local add = BuggyAdditionFunction(2, 3)
print(add)
```

Here, `BuggyAdditionFunction` multiplies the two arguments instead of adding them together. Notice the `debug()` command before the function returns. When this command is hit, control in the console will be given to the debugger. Type `l` and hit *Enter* to print the local variables. Doing so, it's easy to see that `sum` is wrong and needs to be fixed.

Error-handling in Lua

Lua does not officially support exceptions. But, a similar mechanism can be built with pcalls, or protected calls. An exception halts the flow of code in case of an error, and returns control to the caller right away. Furthermore, some kind of error code is likely provided to the caller. This method of raising errors immediately should, in theory, allow callers to handle unsafe code gracefully.

 Much like `debugger.lua`, third-party Lua modules for profiling already exist. Unsurprisingly, one of the best modules for profiling is `profile.lua`. You can learn more about `profile.lua` and download it here: `https://bitbucket.org/itraykov/profile.lua`

pcall and error

Lua's most efficient way to handle errors is `pcall`, or protected call. The `pcall` function takes only one argument, the function to be called. Optionally, if the function takes arguments, they should also be passed to `pcall` as additional arguments. On success, it returns true and all of the values the function would normally return. On failure, it returns false, and any error messages that need to be returned as well.

When an error happens, the `error` function can be used to stop the execution of the current method. The `error` function expects only one argument (and even that's optional): an error message. This message can be a string, but doesn't have to be. The error message can be any valid value. The code here shows a simple use for `pcall` and `error`:

```
function Normalize(x, y, z)
  local dot = x * x + y * y + z * z
  if dot == 0 then
    error("Can't normalize zero vector")
  end
  local len = math.sqrt(dot);
  return x / len, y / len, z / len
```

```
end

local ok, x, y, z = pcall(Normalize, 0, 0, 0)
if not ok then
  print ("Error occured normalizing vector")
  print ("Error message: " .. x)
else
  print ("Vector normalized")
end
```

assert

Errors raised with `pcall` do not interfere with the stability of the program. When an error can be recovered from, it should be handled with `pcall`. But, if an error is catastrophic, it should be handled with `assert`. Unlike `pcall`, `assert` assumes an error is not recoverable and will simply kill the program.

The assert function takes two arguments, a test value and a string. If the test value evaluates to `false` or `nil`, assert will kill the program. If the test value evaluates to anything else, it is returned. The second argument is a string. This string will be printed out as the reason that the program has failed executing. The `normalize` example can be rewritten to use an assertion, like so:

```
function Normalize(x, y, z)
  local dot = x * x + y * y + z * z
  assert(dot ~= 0, "Can't normalize zero vector")
  local len = math.sqrt(dot);
  return x / len, y / len, z / len
end

local x, y, z = Normalize(0, 0, 0)
print("normalized vector")
```

Profiling

Not all Lua debugging is about errors. Sometimes, debugging is more optimization work. In order to tell what part of your code is running slow, or to detect any code hot spots, you have to profile your code. Profiling code means measuring how long something took to execute, or how many times something has executed. We can use Lua's debug library to build a simple profiler.

The profile module

We will implement the profiler as a new module. Create a new file, `profiler.lua`, and declare the `profiler` table. This table will contain four other tables: one table for the names of every function, one for the number of times a function is called, one for the total time spent on the function, and one for timing the functions.

The key to each of these tables is going to be a function object:

```lua
local profiler = {}

profiler.names = { }
profiler.counts = { }
profiler.times = { }
profiler.timers = { }
```

The `profiler` module will have two important public functions: `start` and `stop`. These functions will start and stop the profiler, respectively. The `profiler` module will have an internal function, `private_hook`. The `start` and `stop` functions just set and clear the `private_hook` function as a debug hook. The debug hook will fire for both call and return events:

```lua
profiler.start = function()
  debug.sethook(profiler.private_hook, "c r")
end

profiler.stop = function()
  debug.sethook()
end
```

Once the profiler is done profiling, there needs to be a way to collect and review the data it collected. This is where the `dump` function of the `profiler` comes in. This function will look trough all the records in the profiler and print out their values:

```lua
profiler.dump = function()
  for k, v in pairs(profiler.names) do
    local out = "function " .. v
    out = out .. " was called "
    out = out .. profiler.counts[k]
    out = out .. " times and took "
    out = out .. profiler.times[k]
    out = out .. " seconds to execute"
    print(out)
  end
end
```

Finally, let's take a look at how the `private_hook` function works. This function does all of the actual profiling work. The explanation of this function is going to be broken up into a few sections of code here. First, the function needs to get the debug info of its caller, that is, two levels up the stack. If the caller was not Lua, or if the calling function is `profiler.stop`, the `private_hook` function needs to stop execution:

```
profiler.private_hook = function(event)
  local info = debug.getinfo(2, "fSn")
  if info.what ~= "Lua" then
    return
  end

  local f = info.func
  if f == profiler.stop then
    return
  end
```

Next, we handle the event when a function call is seen for the first time. We know if this is the first time a function is called if it is not in the `profiler.names` table. Additionally, we need to check and make sure the current event is a call event. If both of these conditions are true, default values need to be added to the `profiler.names`, `profiler.counts`, `profiler.times`, and `profiler.timers` tables:

```
if profiler.names[f] == nil and event == "call" then
  profiler.names[f] = info.name
  profiler.counts[f] = 1
  profiler.times[f] = 0.0
  profiler.timers[f] = os.clock()
```

On the other hand, if the `profiler.names[f]` table already contains the function, we know some profiling work has to be done. The profiler needs to do different work based on the event being processed:

- If the event is a call event, the number of times the function has been called needs to be increased, and the timer for the function needs to be set.
- If the event is a return event, the time between the call event and now needs to be calculated, and added to the total running time of the function:

```
elseif profiler.names[f] ~= nil then
  if event == "call" then
    profiler.counts[f] = profiler.counts[f] + 1
    profiler.timers[f] = os.clock()
  elseif event == "return" then
    local t = profiler.times[f];
    local d = os.difftime(
      profiler.timers[f],
```

```
        os.clock()
    )
    profiler.times[f] = t + d
  end
 end
end -- End private_hook function
```

Finally, finish up the module by returning the profiler table:

```
return profiler
```

Using the profile module

The profiler module we just created is straightforward and easy to use. First, you need to include the actual `profiler` module. Whenever you want to start recording functions, call `profiler.start()`. Calling `profiler.stop()` will stop the profiler from collecting further information. To see all of the information that the profiler has collected, call `profiler.dump()`. The following code provides a simple example of how to use the profiler module:

```
profiler = require("profiler")
profiler.start()

function Normalize(x, y, z)
  local dot =
  assert(dot ~= 0, "Can't normalize zero vector")
  local len = math.sqrt(2);
  return x / len, y / len, z / len
end

local x, y, z = Normalize(7, 8, 9)
print("normalized vector")
local x, y, z = Normalize(6, 7, 4)
print("normalized vector")
local x, y, z = Normalize(2, 9, 5)
print("normalized vector")

profiler.stop()
profiler.dump()
```

Integrated development environments

So far, we have covered how to use the built-in features of Lua to debug code. To make debugging easier, several integrated development environments, or IDEs, for Lua exist. An IDE is an external application that can be used to run your Lua code. Typically, IDEs provide syntax highlighting, and sometimes code auto-completion, visual breakpoints, call stacks, and watch windows. This section will cover how to use three of the most popular Lua IDEs.

LuaEdit

LuaEdit is a simple Lua editor that offers a visual studio-like interface with similar functionality and hotkeys. This IDE features breakpoints, a call stack view, and a watch view. LuaEdit provides all the functionality one would look for in a fully featured IDE. The only downside is that LuaEdit is Windows-only. You can download LuaEdit here: `http://luaedit.sourceforge.net`

Breakpoints

The most powerful feature of LuaEdit is being able to set breakpoints. To set a breakpoint, click in the gutter next to the line numbers. A red dot will appear; this is a breakpoint that is now set as shown in the next screenshot. You can click the green arrow or press *F5* to start debugging. The program will run until a breakpoint is hit. You can quit the debugger any time by clicking the blue square, or hitting *Shift + F5*:

As you can see in the previous screenshot, once a breakpoint is hit, the line you are on will turn yellow. You can use the buttons next to **run & stop** to step over the current line, step into the function that is on the current line, or to step out of the current function. Keyboard shortcuts for all of these also exist: they are *F11, F10*, and *Shift + F11*, respectively.

Locals and Watch

There are two important windows that can be opened from **Debug | Window**, and they are *Watch* and *Locals*. Both the **Watch** and **Locals** windows are visible in the screenshot here:

The *Locals* window automatically shows the local variables of the currently executing function. It's very useful for debugging. The **Watch** window works similarly, except you must provide the name of each variable to watch. To do so, double-click on the first empty item's name, and type the name of the variable to watch.

Callstack

The **Callstack** window can be found under **Debug** | **Windows**, and is shown in the following screenshot:

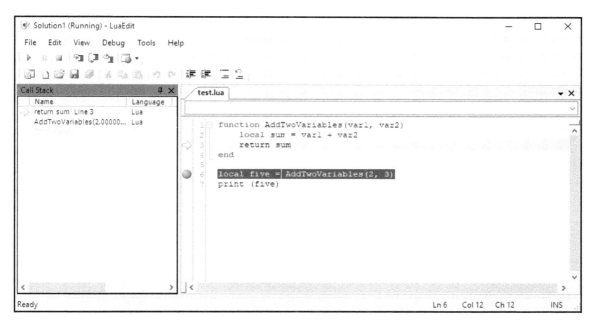

The **Call Stack** window shows the current stack of your program. Every time a function is called, it is put on the **Call Stack**. Using this window you can trace the program's execution from the entry point of Lua to the currently executing function.

Decoda

Decoda is a free and open source Lua IDE, similar to LuaEdit. Decoda was originally developed for the game Natural Selection II. Since then, it has become open source. Decoda offers syntax highlighting, auto completion, breakpoints, watch windows, and call stack viewing. Unlike other IDEs, Decoda patches itself into any executable running a standard Lua distribution. This makes the IDE usable with applications that have no native support for it.

Like LuaEdit, Decoda is a Windows-only program. You can learn more about Decoda and download it here: `https://unknownworlds.com/decoda/`.

Starting debugging

To start debugging with **Decoda**, click on **Edit** | **Start Debugging** or hit *F5*. When debugging code with Decoda, you have to specify a run time. This is a `.exe` file for **Decoda** to hook into. If you're running vanilla Lua, this would be `lua.exe` or `lua52.exe`. You can also configure any command-line arguments and the working directory on this screen, as shown here:

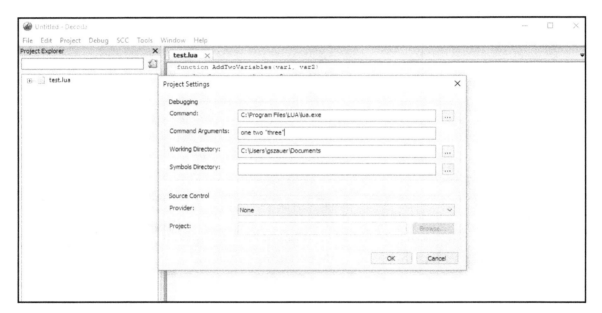

Everything else

Decoda supports the same set of debug features as LuaEdit. In fact, it even uses the same keyboard shortcuts:

The preceding screenshot shows a breakpoint being set, the call stack, a watch window, and the breakpoints window. You can find all of these windows under the *Window* menu item. If you are not familiar with how these windows or breakpoints work, return to the *LuaEdit* section of this chapter.

Zero Brane Studio

Zero Brane Studio offers the standard set of debug tools that LuaEdit and Decoda perform. It can set breakpoints, and has a call stack and a watch window. The big thing that sets Zero Brane apart is its cross platform. The Zero Brane IDE is written in Lua and works on Windows, macOS, and Linux. You can download Zero Brane Studio here: `https://studio.zerobrane.com`

Selecting an interpreter

Zero Brane Studio supports many Lua interpreters for different development environments. You can see all of the interpreters Zero Brane Studio supports from the **Project | Lua Interpreter** menu. The following screenshot shows all of the available interpreters as well:

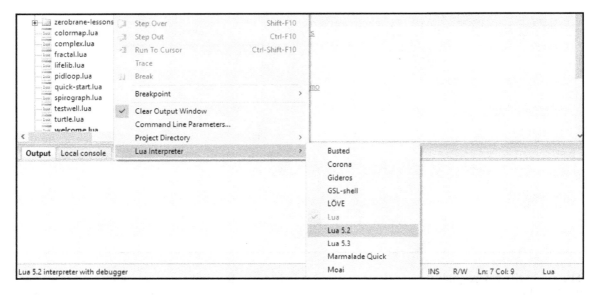

To run the code that is provided in this book, you should use the **Lua 5.2** interpreter option.

Starting the debugger

Because Zero Brane Studio is written in Lua and is cross-platform, it can't automatically hook into an interpreter like LuaEdit or Decoda can. Instead, Zero Brane's debug facilities rely on a Luamodule, much like `debug.lua` discussed earlier in this chapter. To enable debugging in Zero Brane Studio, you need to include the following line of code at the start of your program:

```
require("mobdebug").start()
```

Breakpoints will not work until that code is executed. After that line of code has executed, you should be able to debug in Zero Brane using tools similar to those provided by LuaEdit and Decoda.

Visual Studio Code

Visual Studio Code does not have native support for Lua Debugging. There are some plugins available, such as Lua Debug, that enable debugging of Lua files, but they tend to be Windows-only or require other dependencies. At the time of writing, Lua Debug is the most stable and powerful debugger available in Visual Studio Code. You can download it here: `https://marketplace.visualstudio.com/items?itemName=actboy168.lua-debug`.

Summary

In this chapter, you learned how to use Lua's built-in functionality to gather debug information on the currently running program. Next, error-handling within Lua was covered. Finally, we discussed how to use external programs, IDEs, to write and debug Lua faster. After having read this chapter, you should be ready to use Lua in a production environment.

6
Embedding Lua

So far, we have been using Lua as a standalone language. We did this by using the Lua interpreter, which is the `lua52` program we renamed `lua` in `Chapter 1`, *Introduction to Lua*. The Lua interpreter itself is written in C. In this chapter, we will explore some of the same methods used to create the interpreter.

Lua as a language was designed with C interoperability in mind. You can use Lua as a standalone language or as an embedded scripting language. Many games and other applications utilize Lua as a scripting language—we will see some examples of this in the next chapter.

In this chapter, we're going to focus on some of the common tasks involved in embedding Lua into any C or C++ application. While we are only focusing on the C API, Lua can be embedded into many languages using the same API.

 This chapter assumes you already have some working knowledge of C or C++. This chapter is not intended to be an introduction to C. As such, it only focuses on the Lua C API.

By the end of this chapter, you will be able to do the following:

- Understand the Lua C API
- Understand the Lua stack
- Create Lua variables from C
- Call Lua functions from C
- Call C functions from Lua

Technical requirements

You will be required to have JavaScript programming language. Finally, to use the Git repository of this book, the user needs to install Git.

The code files of this chapter can be found on GitHub:
`https://github.com/PacktPublishing/Lua-Quick-Start-Guide/tree/master/Chapter06`

Check out the following video to see the code in action:
`http://bit.ly/2LC8Xzn`

Working with the C API

The Lua C API is efficient and lightweight. There are a few important header files we need to be familiar with before writing any C code. These files are the following:

- `lua.h`: Provides all the functions needed to work with Lua. All functions in this file are prefixed with `lua_`.
- `luaxlib.h`: Uses the public API exposed in `lua.h` to provide higher levels of abstraction for common tasks. All functions in this file are prefixed with `luaL_`.
- `lualib.h`: Provides the standard Lua libraries. All functions in this file are also prefixed with `luaL_`.

Lua does not allocate any global memory. Instead it stores all of its states in a structure called `lua_State`. This structure contains everything that the Lua runtime needs to operate. Putting a mutex lock around your `lua_State` object is a fast and easy way to make sure any Lua instance is thread safe. It's perfectly valid to create multiple states and therefore multiple Lua runtimes in one application, though the use cases for this are scarce.

To create a new Lua state, call the `luaL_newstate()` function, which will return a pointer to a `lua_State` structure. This pointer needs to be passed to all future Lua API calls—this is how Lua knows what runtime it is working with. After your program is done running, destroy the state with the `lua_close(lua_State*)` function.

When you create a new Lua state, the standard Lua libraries are not automatically loaded. This can be problematic as Lua programmers will expect, as a minimum, that the standard Lua libraries will be available. You can load the standard libraries with the `luaL_openlibs(lua_State*)` function.

The code that follows demonstrates how to set up and destroy an embedded Lua runtime:

```c
#include "lua.h"
#include "lauxlib.h"
#include "lualib.h"

int main(int argc, char** argv) {
  // First, create a new lua state
  lua_State *L = luaL_newstate();
  // Next, load all the standard libraries
  luaL_openlibs(L);

  //Write code that interacts with the Lua runtime here

  // Finally, destory the lua state
  lua_close(L);
  return 0;
}
```

Lua does not add `#ifdef __cplusplus` or extern "C" decorations to it's code. This means Lua can be compiled as C or as C++ code. Since C++ mangles function names, make sure to link to the right version of the library.

The stack

Lua and C are fundamentally different languages. They handle everything differently, such as memory management, types, and even function calls. This poses a problem when trying to integrate the two: how can we communicate between these two languages? This is where the Lua stack comes in.

The Lua stack is an abstract stack that sits between C and the Lua runtime. It's a **Last In First Out (LIFO)** stack. The idea is, both C and Lua know the rules of the stack and so long as they both obey the rules, they can coexist and communicate.

In general, you can think of the stack as a shared data storage mechanism. The way it normally works is that you push some values onto the stack in C. Then, you call a Lua function and hand control over to the Lua runtime. The runtime pops the values off the stack, and the function in question does its work and pushes the return value back on the stack. Control is then handed back to C, which pops the return value off the stack.

The following diagram demonstrates this flow:

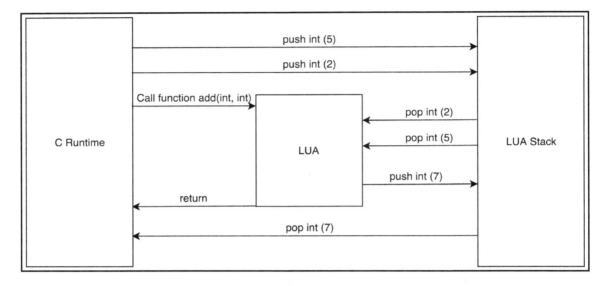

Pushing to the stack

The first step in working with the Lua stack is usually to push some data onto it. The Lua C API provides several functions to push different types of data onto the stack. The following functions can be used to push data:

- `lua_pushnil(lua_State*)`: Pushes nil onto the stack
- `lua_pushboolean(lua_State*, bool)`: Pushes a Boolean value onto the stack
- `lua_pushnumber(lua_State*, lua_Number)`: Pushes a double onto the stack
- `lua_pushinteger(lua_State*, lua_Integer)`: Pushes a signed integer onto the stack
- `lua_pushstring (lua_State*, const char*)`: Pushes a NULL terminated string onto the stack

When you push a string onto the stack, Lua creates its own copy of that string. As soon as the push operation is finished, you can modify or even free the copy of the string you have.

The stack is not infinite. Before pushing data onto the stack, it's a good idea to check whether there is actually room for the data or not. To check how much room the stack has, you can use the `int lua_checkstack(lua_State*, int)` function. The function takes two arguments: the Lua state and the number of items you want to add to the stack. If there is enough room, the function returns `true (1)`. If there is not enough room, the function returns `false (0)`. This function *may* actually grow the stack if needed.

Querying the stack

Lua references elements in the stack using indices. The bottom element of the stack is index 1; the indices grow towards the top of the stack where the last element was added. Lua can also index the stack in reverse. An index of −1 refers to the top of the stack, −2 to the element right below the top, and so on:

Lua Stack
Item 2, valid indices: 3, -1
Item 1, valid indices: 2, -2
Item 0, valid indices: 1, -3

Using indices, you can check the type of any element on the stack. The functions listed here can be used to query the type of element on the stack. They all return `true (1)` or `false (0)`. Each function takes a Lua state for its first argument and a stack index for its second:

- `int lua_isnumber(lua_State*, int)`: Checks whether the element at the provided index is a number
- `int lua_isstring(lua_State*, int)`: Checks whether the element at the provided index is a string
- `int lua_isboolean(lua_State*, int)`: Checks whether the element at the provided index is a Boolean
- `int lua_istable(lua_State*, int)`: Checks whether the element at the provided index is a table
- `int lua_isnil(lua_State*, int)`: Checks whether the element at the provided index is `nil`

There is a similar function, `int lua_type(lua_State*, int)`, which returns an enumeration value with the type of object. This function can be useful when used in a switch statement or something similar. The following are valid enumeration values that the function could return:

- `LUA_TNUMBER`: Represents a Lua number
- `LUA_TSTRING`: Represents a Lua string
- `LUA_TBOOLEAN`: Represents a Lua Boolean
- `LUA_TTABLE`: Represents a Lua table
- `LUA_TNIL`: Represents `nil`

Reading from the stack

Lua provides several functions to retrieve values from the stack. The most common functions are listed here. The first argument to each of these functions is the Lua state, and the second argument is an integer, the index of the element being read:

- `int lua_toboolean(lua_State*, int)`: Returns `true` (1) or `false` (0).
- `lua_Number lua_tonumber(lua_State*, int)`: Returns a double.
- `lua_Integer lua_tointeger(lua_State*, int)`: Returns an integer.
- `const char* lua_tostring(lua_State*, int, size_t*)`: Returns a pointer to the internal Lua string. The last parameter is optional; if it's not `NULL`, the size of the string will be written to it.
- `size_t lua_objlen(lua_State*, int)`: Returns the same value as the # operator in Lua.

When calling `lua_tostring`, the function returns the pointer to an internal string. The return value is `const`, to remind you that you should not modify this value! As soon as the value is popped off the stack, that string might no longer exist. It's a bad idea to hold on to the return value of this function—instead, make a copy and store it.

Stack size

You can get the index of the top element of the Lua stack with the `int lua_gettop(lua_State*)` function. The value this function returns will be the index of the top element on the Lua stack.

You can set the top element (size) of the stack with `lua_settop(lua_State*, int)`. This function returns nothing. The second argument is the element that should be the index of the new top element on the stack. This function effectively resizes the stack.

If the requested stack size with `lua_settop` is smaller than the previous size, all elements above the new top are simply discarded. If the requested stack size is greater than the previous one, all new elements will be filled with `nil`.

There is a `lua_pop(lua_State*, int)` macro defined in `lua.h`, which is a handy shortcut. This function will pop some elements off the stack, simply discarding them. The second argument of the function is how many elements to remove.

Reading Lua variables from C

It's very easy to read and write Lua variables from C. Because of this, Lua is often used as a configuration language or to save and load the state of a program. The Lua runtime will parse and interpret files for you, removing the need for manual parsing. And the syntax of Lua lends itself very well to these kinds of tasks. In this section, we're going to explore how to read Lua variables that are used as configuration data.

Loading a Lua file

To read a Lua variable in C, you will need to load the Lua file with `int luaL_loadfile(lua_State*, const char*)`. The resulting chunk will then need to be executed with `lua_pcall(lua_State*, int, int, int, int)`. After the Lua chunk is loaded and executed, any variables it declared can be read. The `lua_pcall` function will be described in more detail in the *Calling Lua functions from C* section of this chapter.

The `luaL_loadfile` function returns 0 on success, or one of the following enumerations on failure: `LUA_ERRSYNTAX`, `LUA_ERRMEM`, `LUA_ERRFILE`. The first argument to the function is the Lua state to work with, the second is the file path to load. The resulting Lua chunk is added to the Lua stack.

The `lua_pcall` function is intended to execute Lua chunks, which are most often functions. This function will return 0 on success and an error code if it fails. In addition, if the function fails, an error message will be pushed onto the stack.

The first argument of `lua_pcall` is the Lua state to operate on. The second argument is the number of arguments the chunk being called expects. This argument is only used when calling Lua functions and should match the number of function parameters. When executing a chunk that is loaded from a file (or a string), this argument should be 0.

The third argument of `lua_pcall` is the number of results the chunk is expected to return. The number specified here is the number of items `lua_pcall` will leave on the stack. If there is a number here, you are responsible for reading and removing those values from the stack. When loading a simple file chunk, this value can be 0. Some files (such as modules) return a table or multiple values. In those cases, the value should not be 0.

The fourth and final argument of `lua_pcall` is the error handler. A value of 0 tells Lua to push the error message onto the stack if `lua_pcall` fails.

Reading global variables

Reading a global variable is done in three steps. You have to use the name of the variable to push its value onto the stack. Once on the stack, the value can be read by C. After you have the value in C, clean up the stack by removing the old copy.

You can push a global variable onto the stack by name using the `lua_getglobal (lua_State*, const char *)` function. The first argument of `lua_getglobal` is the Lua state. The second argument is the name of the variable to push it onto the stack. This function does not return anything.

The `lua_getglobal` function uses the name of a global variable to leave its value on the stack. To read the value in C, you have to use one of the `lua_to` functions such as `lua_tonumber` or `lua_tostring`. These functions were discussed in the *Reading from the stack* section of this chapter. Once you have the value of the variable in C, clean up the stack by calling `lua_pop`.

Example

Let's see a simple example of how to read variables from Lua into C. Consider the use case where we create a game character. We want to store the attributes of that character in an external configuration file to allow for easy editing. The attributes file will look something like this:

```
class = "Warrior"
attack = 56
defense = 43
```

Reading the configuration values in C would involve creating a new Lua state, loading the Lua file, pushing each variable onto the stack, reading and storing the values, and finally popping all of the values off the stack. The following code demonstrates how to do this:

```c
#include "lua.h"
#include "lauxlib.h"
#include "lualib.h"
#include <string.h>

int main(int argc, char** argv) {
    lua_State *L = luaL_newstate();
    luaL_openlibs(L);

    // Load the file "hero.lua"
    int result = luaL_loadfile(L, "hero.lua");
    if (result != 0) {
        printf("Could not load hero.lua, exiting");
        lua_close(L);
        return -1;
    }

    // Execute the loaded Lua chunk
    result = lua_pcall(L, 0, 0, 0);
    if (result != 0) {
        const char* error = lua_tostring(L, -1);
        printf("Error loading hero.lua, exiting.\n");
        printf("Error message %s", error);
        lua_close(L);
        return -1;
    }
```

```
    int stack_base = lua_gettop(L);

    // Push character attributes onto stack
    lua_getglobal(L, "class"); // Index 1
    lua_getglobal(L, "attack"); // Index 2
    lua_getglobal(L, "defense"); // Index 3

    // Read the value of each new thing on the stack
    const char* class_p = lua_tostring(L, stack_base + 1);
    char class_sz[32];
    strcpy(class_sz, class_p);
    int attack = lua_tointeger(L, stack_base + 2);
    int defense = lua_tointeger(L, stack_base + 3);

    // Clean up the stack
    lua_pop(L, 3);

    // Do something with the values
    printf("Character is %s with %d attack and %d defense\n", class_sz,
attack, defense);

    // Close Lua & clean up
    lua_close(L);
    return 0;
}
```

The preceding sample code gets the base index of the stack before anything is pushed to it and then reads values using offsets from that base index. You should never assume that the stack is empty—don't hard code indices. Instead, always use indices relative to a known offset.

Creating Lua variables from C

Communicating with Lua is one way. In addition to reading Lua variables from C, you can also create Lua variables from C. The process for doing so is simple: you push a value onto the stack, then tell the Lua runtime to assign that value to a variable by name.

To create a variable, use the `lua_setglobal (lua_State*, const char*)` function. This function returns nothing. Its first argument is the Lua state to work on, the second argument is the name of the global variable to assign. This function will pop the top value off the stack and assign it to the name of the variable specified.

Let's take the example from the last section and reverse it. This time, the variables for class, attack, and defense are going to be created in C and printed out in Lua. The C code will push all values onto the stack, then use `lua_setglobal` to assign them to variables. After the variables are set up, a Lua file should be loaded and executed:

```
#include "lua.h"
#include "lauxlib.h"
#include "lualib.h"

int main(int argc, char** argv) {
    lua_State *L = luaL_newstate();
    luaL_openlibs(L);

    // Push values
    lua_pushstring(L, "Warrior");
    lua_pushnumber(L, 56);
    lua_pushnumber(L, 43);

    // Assign from top of stack, IE reverse order
    lua_setglobal(L, "defense");
    lua_setglobal(L, "attack");
    lua_setglobal(L, "class");

    // Load the file "printinfo.lua"
    int result = luaL_loadfile(L, "printinfo.lua");
    if (result != 0) {
        printf("Could not load hero.lua, exiting");
        lua_close(L);
        return -1;
    }

    // Execute the loaded Lua chunk
    result = lua_pcall(L, 0, 0, 0);
    if (result != 0) {
        const char* error = lua_tostring(L, -1);
        printf("Error loading hero.lua, exiting.\n");
        printf("Error message %s", error);
        lua_close(L);
        return -1;
    }

    lua_close(L);
    return 0;
}
```

Next, the `printinfo.lua` file will be responsible for printing out all of these values. Notice the variables `class`, `attack`, and `defense` are never created in Lua. They can be referenced because they were created in C:

```
print ("Charater is " .. class .. " with " .. attack .. " attack and " ..
defense .. " defense");
```

Calling Lua functions from C

The method for calling Lua functions from C has already been covered in the *Loading a Lua file* section of this chapter—it's `lua_pcall`. This time around, we will be using the second and third arguments of the function. As a reminder, the second argument is the number of arguments on the stack for Lua to consume, and the third argument is the number of values we expect Lua to leave on the stack for us.

Let's make an example function in Lua that takes two numbers and returns a linear index into a matrix. Only the Lua code will know the width of the matrix. The Lua code for finding this linear index will look something like this:

```
num_columns = 7
function GetIndex(row, col)
    return row * num_columns + col
end
```

The preceding Lua function expects two variables to be on the stack: `row` and `col`. It will leave one value on the stack. Next, let's create a C wrapper function that has a similar name and signature. This wrapper function is expected to run in a valid Lua context that has loaded the Lua file with the function already defined in the preceding code:

```
int LinearIndex(lua_State*L, int row, int col) {
    // Push the GetIndex function on the stack
    lua_getglobal(L, "GetIndex");
    // Stack: function (GetIndex)
    // Push the row variable on the stack
    lua_pushnumber(L, row);
    // Stack: function (GetIndex), int (row)

    // Push the col variable on the stack
    lua_pushnumber(L, col);
    // Stack: function (GetIndex), int (row), int (col)

    // Pop two arguments off the stack (row & col)
    // Call the function on the top of the stack (GetIndex)
    // Leave one value on the stack
```

```
lua_pcall(L, 2, 1, 0);
// Stack: int (return value of GetIndex)

// Remove the result of GetIndex from the stack
int result = lua_tointeger(L, -1);
lua_pop(L, 1);
// Stack: empty

return result;
}
```

Calling C functions from Lua

Because functions in C and Lua work so differently, exposing a C function to Lua can get a bit tricky. All C functions that Lua can call must follow the signature of `lua_CFunction`, which is defined in `lua.h` as the following:

```
typedef int (*lua_CFunction) (lua_State *L);
```

This function takes only one argument, the `lua_State`. The return value of the function is an integer. This integer is the number of elements that the function pushed onto the stack as return values.

 Lua has multiple stacks—each C function called from Lua has its own stack and does not share the global stack.

Let's take for example a simple C function that returns the magnitude of a three-dimensional vector. In C, the code for doing so might look something like the following:

```
double Vec3Magnitude(double x, double y, double z) {
    double dot = x * x + y * y + z * z;
    if (dot == 0.0) {
        return 0.0;
    }
    return sqrt(dot);
}
```

The preceding function can't be exposed to Lua directly because it doesn't follow the `lua_CFunction` signature. There are two ways to expose this function, either to re-write it or to write a wrapper function for it. Both approaches are similar. The following is a rewritten example:

```
int LuaVec3Magnitude(lua_State* L) {
    double x = lua_tonumber(L, 3);
    double y = lua_tonumber(L, 2);
    double z = lua_tonumber(L, 1);

    lua_pop(L, 3);

    double dot = x * x + y * y + z * z;
    if (dot == 0.0) {
        lua_pushnil(L);
    }
    else {
        lua_pushnumber(L, sqrt(dot));
    }

    return 1;
}
```

The preceding function can be called from Lua. Before being called, it must be *registered*. Registering a function means it first needs to be pushed onto the stack with the `lua_pushcfunction` function. Next, the function on the stack needs to be assigned to a variable with `lua_setglobal`. The code that follows registers the `LuaVec3Magnitude` function to be available in Lua:

```
lua_pushcfunction(L, LuaVec3Magnitude);
lua_setglobal(L, "Vec3Magnitude");
```

After the `LuaVec3Magnitude` function is registered as `Vec3Magnitude` in Lua, it can be called at any time.

Rewriting a function is not always possible, but you can still write a wrapper function. For example, we could create a function called `LuaWrapperVec3Magnitude` that interfaces with Lua, but instead of doing the work of `Vec3Magnitude`, it just calls the `Vec3Magnitude` function. Then, we can expose `LuaWrapperVec3Magnitude` as `Vec3Magnitude` to Lua.

The following code demonstrates this:

```
int LuaWrapperVec3Magnitude(lua_State* L) {
    double x = lua_tonumber(L, 3);
    double y = lua_tonumber(L, 2);
    double z = lua_tonumber(L, 1);

    lua_pop(L, 3);

    // Call the original function so it is responsible
    // for doing the actual work
    double result = Vec3Magnitude(x, y, z);

    if (dot == 0.0) {
        lua_pushnil(L);
    }
    else {
        lua_pushnumber(L, result);
    }

    return 1;
}

// Code to expose the wrapper function:
lua_pushcfunction(L, LuaWrapperVec3Magnitude);
lua_setglobal(L, "Vec3Magnitude");
```

Working with tables in C

Up until now, we have only been working with basic Lua types and functions. Lua's C API also allows us to work with tables. A new table can be created with the `lua_newtable (lua_State*)` function. This function returns nothing and only takes the Lua state as an argument. The `lua_newtable` function will create an empty table and leave it on top of the stack. Once the table is on the stack, it's up to you to assign it to a variable. For example, the following code creates a table named `"vector"` that has global scope:

```
lua_newtable(L);
lua_setglobal(L, "vector");
```

The C API for working with tables can get a little verbose. There are a few libraries that address this and aim to reduce the amount of code you have to actually type. One such library, Lua Bridge, will be discussed in Chapter 7, *Lua Bridge*.

After the table is created, you will be able to get and set values to and from the table. However, to do so, the table will need to be on the stack. You can retrieve tables to be on the stack, just like any other variable type, by using lua_getglobal.

Reading values from a table

Fields from a table can be retrieved with the lua_gettable (lua_State*, int) function. This function returns nothing; its first argument is the Lua state to work on. Typically, accessing a table in Lua involves both the table and a key, for example: tbl[key]. Using lua_gettable, the table (tbl) is expected to be at the index specified by the second variable. The key (key) is expected to be on the top of the stack. The following code demonstrates how to retrieve the value of the key x from a table named vector:

```
lua_getglobal(L, "vector");
lua_pushstring(L, "x");
lua_gettable(L, -2);
```

Since retrieving a variable is so common, Lua provides a handy shortcut function, lua_getfield (lua_State*, int, const char*). This helper function avoids having to push the name of the key onto the stack, and instead takes it as the third argument. The second argument is still the index of the table on the stack. The preceding example could be rewritten with lua_getfield like, as follows:

```
// Push vector to the top of the stack
lua_getglobal(L, "vector");
// The index -1 refers to vector, which is on top of the stack
// Leaves the value of x on the top of the stack
lua_getfield(L, -1, "x");
// The stack has 2 new values (vector & x)on it that will need to be
cleaned up at some point
```

You might have noticed that the preceding code passes a negative index to lua_getfield. Recall from the *Querying the stack* section of this chapter that positive numbers index the stack from the bottom up, while negative numbers index the stack from the top down.

Passing −1 in the previous code works because the `lua_getglobal` function call will leave the `"vector"` table on the top of the stack. At this point, we don't know (or care) how large the stack is, just that the top element is the table `"vector"`. After calling `lua_getfield`, the value of `"x"` is on the top of the stack.

Writing values to a table

Lua offers the `lua_settable (lua_State*, int)` function to set fields in a table. The function returns nothing. Its first argument is the Lua state to work on and the second argument is the index of a table on the stack.

The value being set is expected to be on top of the stack, and the key to set it to is expected to be just below that. `lua_settable` will pop both the key and value off the stack, but it will leave the table on the stack.

For example, the Lua code `vector["y"] = 7` could be written with this API as follows:

```
// Push vector onto the stack
lua_gettable(L, "vector");
// Push y onto the stack
lua_pushstring(L, "y");
// Push 7 onto the stack
lua_pushnumber(L, 7);
// The stack has three new variables on it
// The index of 7 is -1
// The index of "y" is -2
// The index of "vector" is -3

// Call lua_settable on the "vector" table at index -3
lua_settable(L, -3);

// lua_settable will pop the key ("y") and value (7) off the stack
// Only one item is left on the stack, the "vector" table
// The item left on the stack should be cleaned up at some point
```

Lua also offers the `lua_setfield (lua_State*, int, const char*)` function which avoids the need to push the key onto the stack. The first two arguments are the same as `lua_settable`. The third argument is the key of what is being set.

The value of what is being set is expected to be at the top of the stack. The `lua_setfield` function will pop the value off the stack, much like `lua_settable` does.

The preceding code sample can be rewritten to use `lua_setfield` as follows:

```
// Push "vector" onto the stack
lua_gettable(L, "vector");
// Push 7 onto the stack
lua_pushnumber(L, 7);
// Call lua_setfield on the "vector"table at index -2
lua_setfield(L, -2, "y");

// lua_setfield will pop the value (7) off the stack
// Only one item is left on the stack, the "vector" table
```

Meta tables

You can both test whether a table has a meta table and retrieve the said meta table with the `int lua_getmetatable (lua_State*, int)` function. The first argument to this function is the Lua state it affects, and the second argument is the index of a table on the stack. If the table at the specified index has no meta table, the `lua_getmetatable` function returns 0 and does not push anything onto the stack. If the table at the specified index does have a meta table, the `lua_getmetatable` function will return 1 and push the meta table onto the stack.

You can assign a meta table to an existing table with the `int lua_setmetatable (lua_State*, int)` function. This function takes the Lua state it affects as its first argument, and the index of a table on the stack as the second. It expects the top of the stack to be the meta table and will pop it off the stack. If it can assign the meta table, the function will return 1. Otherwise, if an error occurs, the function will return 0.

User data

Lua has a special data type called userdata. Userdata can store arbitrary C data structures as Lua data—it's just some arbitrary amount of memory. Userdata can have meta tables, which enables us to extend the type using the same mechanism we would use to extend tables. Like tables, userdata is compared by reference, not by value.

To create a new block of userdata memory, use the `void* lua_newuserdata (lua_State*, size_t)` function. The first argument of this function is the Lua state to work on, and the second argument is the number of bytes to reserve for user data. The function returns a pointer to the block of memory that Lua has reserved for this user data.

A three-dimensional vector might be stored in userdata like as follows:

```
struck Vec3 {
    float x, y, z;
}

int make_up_vector(lua_State *L) {
    Vec3* newVec = (Vev3*)lua_newuserdata(L, sizeof(Vec3));
    newVec->x = 0;
    newVec->y = 1;
    newVec->z = 0;
    // The new user data is on the stack
    return 1;
}
```

User data can be retrieved using the `lua_touserdata` function. This function returns a pointer to the user data memory. It's first argument is the Lua state to work on, and the second argument is the index on the stack at which the user data is expected to be. If you modify the pointer returned by the user data, you are modifying the actual value of the user data. The following code sample shows how to use the `lua_touserdata` function:

```
int lua_vec3_cross (lua_State *L) {
    Vec3* a = (Vec3*)lua_touserdata(L, -2);
    Vec3* b = (Vec3*)lua_touserdata(L, -1);

    float dot = a->x * b->x + a->y * b->y + a->z * b->z;
    lua_pushnumber(L, dot);

    return 1;
}
```

Lua C API reference

By now, you have probably noticed that working with the Lua stack can get a bit confusing. Some functions push and pop values onto the stack and others don't. You can find out how each function manipulates the stack by reading through the Lua reference manual, available at: https://www.lua.org/manual/5.2/.

If you scroll down the manual page a bit, every Lua function is listed. Clicking on any of the C API functions will show the signature of the function, a description of how the function works, and some stack information. The manual page for the `lua_setfield` function as follows:

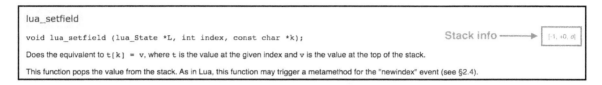

lua_setfield

```
void lua_setfield (lua_State *L, int index, const char *k);
```

Stack info ⟶ [-1, +0, e]

Does the equivalent to t[k] = v, where t is the value at the given index and v is the value at the top of the stack.

This function pops the value from the stack. As in Lua, this function may trigger a metamethod for the "newindex" event (see §2.4).

The stack information is called out in the upper right of the function. There are always three entries in this information box. The first one is how many elements the function removes from the stack, the second number is how many elements the function adds to the stack, and the third entry describes how the function handles errors. Valid values for this third entry are the following:

- −: The function will not raise any errors
- m: The function may raise memory-related errors
- e: The function can raise any error
- v: The function may raise an error on purpose

Summary

In this chapter, we covered how to use the C API to embed Lua into C applications. This allowed us to call Lua functions from C, call C functions from Lua, and to interact between the two languages. At the core of this Lua to C interaction is the Lua stack. The only drawback to Lua's C API is that it can be rather verbose at times. In Chapter 7, *Lua Bridge*, we will cover how to use Lua Bridge, a Lua binding framework that removes a lot of the verbose boilerplate code.

7
Lua Bridge

The Lua C API is verbose and it can sometimes be a bit complicated to navigate. Furthermore, if you are programming in C++, the API doesn't really fit into the OOP idiom. There are a few binding libraries that try to bridge this gap. One of the most intuitive and easy-to-use libraries out there is Lua Bridge. You can get Lua Bridge from GitHub at `https://github.com/vinniefalco/LuaBridge`.

Lua Bridge is a C++ API. When using Lua Bridge, you have to use a C++ compiler.

Lua Bridge focuses on letting the user create object-oriented Lua bindings in an intuitive and easy manner. In fact, using Lua Bridge, you can create a fairly complex Lua class with far less code than if you were writing it using the Lua C API alone. One of the nice features of Lua Bridge is the concept of a **namespace**. A namespace is just a container table that all variables are registered in, like a module. Because of this namespace concept, Lua Bridge will never allocate global variables directly.

The Lua Bridge reference manual can be found online, at `http://vinniefalco.github.io/LuaBridge/Manual.html`.

By the end of this chapter, you will be able to do the following:

- Understand the Lua Bridge API
- Use Lua Bridge to expose C++ classes
- Instantiate C++ classes in Lua
- Call C++ functions from Lua
- Access Lua variables through `LuaRef` objects
- Call Lua functions using `LuaRef` objects

Technical requirements

You will be required to have JavaScript programming language. Finally, to use the Git repository of this book, the user needs to install Git.

The code files of this chapter can be found on GitHub:
`https://github.com/PacktPublishing/Lua-Quick-Start-Guide/tree/master/Chapter07`

Check out the following video to see the code in action:
`http://bit.ly/2JUm2iE`

API conventions

Most functions that are used to register classes or data in the Lua Bridge API return some kind of class. This is done with the intention of allowing functions to be chained. Chaining functions means using the result of one function and calling another function on it.

For example, a member function of an object might return the object, so a different function can be called without storing the actual object as a variable. Consider the following class:

```
class Foo {
public:
  // Assume foo is a singleton
  static Foo* GetInstance();
  Foo* DoWork();
  Foo* PrintResults();
};
```

In the preceding code, the `GetInstance`, `DoWork`, and `PrintResults` functions all return a pointer to the object that they were called on. This lets us get the object, do some work on it, and print the result of that work with only one line of code, as follows:

```
Foo::GetInstance()->DoWork()->PrintResults();
```

Lua Bridge does something very similar. A typical class definition using Lua Bridge usually looks like the following code:

```
getGlobalNamespace(L).beginNamespace("Math").beginClass<Vector>("Vector")
```

To make the code samples easier to read, we will indent chained function calls. The preceding line of code can be indented as follows:

```
getGlobalNamespace(L)
    .beginNamespace("Math")
        .beginClass<Vector>("Vector")
```

Namespaces

Everything inside Lua Bridge must be declared within a namespace. These namespaces have no connection to C++ namespaces, and within Lua, they are just tables. The concept of a namespace is similar to the concept of a Lua module being loaded as a table.

A global namespace exists, and you can register functions, variables, and classes to that namespace, but it's considered bad practice. You can get the global namespace with the following call:

```
getGlobalNamespace(lua_State*)
```

Once you have the global namespace, you can create your own namespace inside it with the `beginNamespace(const char*)` call. This function takes a string with the name of the namespace as an argument. Once you are done working with the namespace, you must close it with the `endNameSpace()` call. If you want to add more classes in different parts of the code in a namespace, it can be opened multiple times. The following code sample demonstrates this:

```
getGlobalNamespace(L)
    .beginNamespace("foo")
      // Add things to foo
    .endNamespace()

// More code
getGlobalNamespace(L)
    .beginNamespace("foo")
      // Add more things to foo
    .endNamespace()
```

If you were to make a variable named `bar` inside the preceding `foo` namespace, accessing the `bar` variable would require using the namespace as follows:

```
print("bar: " .. foo.bar)
```

Variables

The simplest data to register within a namespace is a variable. Variables can be registered with the `addVariable (char const*, T*, bool isWritable)` function. This function is templated, meaning that any type of variable can be added using the function. The first argument to this function is the name that Lua will call the variable, the second is a pointer to the C++ variable. The third argument is optional. When set to `true` (the default value), the variable can be read from and written to, and when set to `false`, the variable becomes read-only.

The following code demonstrates how to register a variable with Lua Bridge:

```
int bar;

getGlobalNamespace(L)
    .beginNamespace("foo")
        .addVariable("bar", &bar)
    .endNamespace()
```

Functions

Global functions can be registered with Lua Bridge as well. These functions don't need to have the same signature as `lua_CFunction`; as Lua Bridge will generate the required glue code. Functions can be exposed with the `addFunction` function. This function takes two arguments. The first one is the Lua-side name of the function, and the second is a pointer to the function. The following code demonstrates how to do this:

```
int bar() {
    return 2;
}

getGlobalNamespace(L)
    .beginNamespace("foo")
        .addFunction("bar", bar)
    .endNamespace()
```

It is also possible to register functions written against the Lua C API that match the signature of `lua_CFunction`. You will most often do this if you need to port some legacy code over, in order to use Lua Bridge. Adding these functions works almost the same; the only difference is that the name of the function to add these types of functions is `addCFunction`. The following code demonstrates how to do this:

```
int bar(lua_State* L) {
    lua_pushnumber(L, 2);
    return 1;
}

getGlobalNamespace(L)
    .beginNamespace("foo")
        .addCFunction("bar", bar)
    .endNamespace()
```

Properties

A property is a mix between a function and a variable. Properties are similar to C#'s getter/setter system. To Lua, a property looks like a normal variable, but every time that variable is read, a function is called. Similarly, every time the variable is changed, a function is called. These are getter/setter functions. If a property has a getter function but no setter, it is effectively read-only.

A property can be added with the `addProperty (char const*, TG (T::*) () const, void (T::*)` function. This function takes three arguments. The first one is the Lua name for the variable, and the second and third arguments are getter and setter functions, respectively. The `addProperty` function has an overloaded version that only takes a getter function. The following code demonstrates how to use properties:

```
int bar;
int get_bar () const {
    // Potentially do some error checking?
    return bar;
}

void set_bar (int b) {
    bar = b;
}
```

```
getGlobalNamespace(L)
    .beginNamespace("foo")
        .addProperty("bar", get_bar, set_bar)
        .addProperty("bar_readonly", get_bar)
    .endNamespace()
```

Classes

The `beginClass/endClass` functions can be used to expose classes to Lua. The class type must be provided as a template argument to the `beginClass` function. You can call `beingClass/endClass` multiple times for the same class, and on each call, new methods and variables can be added. Suppose that a class named Vec3 exists, to represent a 3D vector. It can be exposed to Lua using Lua Bridge, as follows:

```
class Vec3 { };

getGlobalNamespace(L)
    .beginNamespace("Math")
        .beginClass<Vec3>("Vec3")
        .endClass()
    .endNamespace()
```

To create a new object, just call the name of the class as a function. For example, the preceding code can create a new Vec3 with the following code:

```
local vector = Math.Vec3()
```

Constructor

Lua Bridge only supports a single constructor. Overloaded constructors are not possible to declare with Lua Bridge. A constructor can be added with the `addConstructor` function. The function signature of the constructor must be specified as a template argument, since a class may have multiple overloaded constructors. The following code shows a C++ class with three constructors, but only the one that takes three floats is exposed to Lua:

```
class Vec3 {
  public:
    Vec3();
    Vec3(const Vec3& other);
    Vec3(float x, float y, float z);
}
```

```
getGlobalNamespace(L)
    .beginNamespace("Math")
      .beginClass<Vec3>("Vec3")
        .addConstructor<void (*) (float, float, float)>()
      .endClass()
    .endNamespace();
```

Subclass

Classes can be subclassed using Lua Bridge. The base class does not need to be exposed to Lua, only the subclass does. Subclasses can be exposed to Lua Bridge using the `deriveClass` method. Unlike `beginClass`, `deriveClass` should only be called once. Because of the loosely typed nature of Lua and the limitations placed on `deriveClass`, it's usually better to expose classes with `beginClass`, instead. For the sake of completeness, the following code sample illustrates how to use `deriveClass`:

```
class Foo {
    int x;
    int y;
}

class Bar : public Foo {
    int x;
};

getGlobalNamespace(L)
    .beginNamespace("Sample")
        .beginClass<Foo>("Foo")
        .endClass()
        .deriveClass<Bar, Foo>("Bar")
        .endClass()
    .endNameSpace();
```

Member variables, properties, and functions

Adding variables, properties, and functions to a class in Lua Bridge is done in the same fashion as adding any of these things to a namespace. The functions are `addData`, `addFunction`, and `addProperty`. None of these functions require any template data, but the data they point to does have to be scoped to the class it belongs to. The following code sample shows how to use these methods:

```
class Vec3 {
  public:
```

```
        float x, y, z;

    float Magnitude() const;
    void Normalize();
}

getGlobalNamespace(L)
    .beginNamespace("Math")
        .beginClass<Vec3>("Vec3")
            .addData("x", &Vec3::x)
            .addData("y", &Vec3::y)
            .addData("z", &Vec3::z)
            .addProperty("Magnitude", &Vec3::Magnitude)
            .addFunction("Normalize", &Vec3::Normalize)
        .endClass()
    .endNameSpace();
```

Static variables, properties, and functions

Static variables, properties, and functions can be added in the same way that member
variables, properties, and functions can. The function calls to do so
are `addStaticData`, `addStaticProperty`, and `addStaticFunction`.

The following code sample shows how to use all three of these functions:

```
class Vec3 {
  public:
    static Vec3 zero;
    static Vec3 get_upvector() {
        return Vec3(0, 1, 0);
    }

    static Vec3 Cross(Vec3 v1, Vec3 v2);
}

getGlobalNamespace(L)
    .beginNamespace("Math")
        .beginClass<Vec3>("Vec3")
            .addStaticData("Zero", &Vec3::zero, false)
            .addStaticProperty("Up", &Vec3::get_upvector)
            .addStaticFunction("Cross", &Vec3::Cross)
        .endClass()
    .endNameSpace();
```

Calling C functions from Lua

All of the code that we have written so far has been about exposing C to Lua using Lua Bridge. Any C function exposed through Lua Bridge can be called from Lua. If a function is in a namespace and not a class, it is called with the dot syntax: `Math.Sqrt(16)`. But, if a function is in a class, it needs to be called with the colon syntax: `vector:Normalize()`. The following code shows how to expose a C function to Lua and how to call it from Lua.

The C code needs to declare the appropriate vector 3 class, a `Normalize` member function, and a global `dot` product function. Next, the `Register` function exposes all of these functions to Lua, using Lua Bridge:

```
class Vec3 {
  public:
    float x, y, z;
    float Normalize() {
        float dot = x * x + y * y + z * z;
        if (dot == 0) {
            return 0;
        }
        return sqrt(dot);
    }
}

float Dot(Vec3 a, Vec3 b) {
    return a.x * b.x + a.y * b.y + a.z * b.z;
}

void Register(lua_State* L) {
    getGlobalNamespace(L)
        .beginNamespace("Math")
            .beginClass<Vec3>("Vec3")
                .addData("x", &Vec3::x)
                .addData("y", &Vec3::y)
                .addData("z", &Vec3::z)
                .addFunction("Normalize", &Vec3::Normalize)
            .endClass()
            .addFunction("Dot", Dot)
        .endNameSpace();
}
```

The Lua file can create new vectors, and can then set the x, y, or z members of each vector. Then, the Dot and Normalize functions can be called. The following code sample does this:

```
local a = Math.Vec3()
local b = Math.Vec3()

a.x = 7
b.x = 3

print ("Dot: " .. Dot(a, b));

print ("Normalize both");
a:Normalize()
b:Normalize()

print ("Dot: " .. Dot(a, b));
```

LuaRef

Lua Bridge is not just a one-way street, after all, it is a bridge. To read Lua values in C, Lua Bridge provides the LuaRef class. A LuaRef variable can hold any value that a Lua variable can. The getGlobal(lua_State*, const char*) function will return any global Lua variable as a LuaRef value. Consider the following Lua code:

```
foo = "Hello, world"
bar = 42
debug = function()
    print (foo .. " & " .. bar)
end
```

These variables can be retrieved in C or C++ by using the getGlobal function. A LuaRef object can even be called as a function, if it is assigned to one. The following code demonstrates this:

```
LuaRef foo = getGlobal(L, "foo");
LuaRef bar = getGlobal(L, "bar");
LuaRef debug = getGlobal(L, "debug");
bar = 57;
debug();
```

LuaRef variables have a `cast<T>` member function that will convert a given `LuaRef` value into whatever it is being cast to. The following code sample demonstrates this:

```
LuaRef foo = getGlobal(L, "foo");
printf("foo: %s \n", foo.cast<const char*>());
```

LuaRef and tables

A `LuaRef` variable can point to any type of data—even a table! When a `LuaRef` variable points to a table, it can be indexed very naturally using brackets (`[]`). Consider the following Lua code:

```
velocity = {
    x = 7,
    y = 0,
    units = "miles"
}

velocity.debug = function()
    print (velocity.x .. ", " .. velocity.y .. " " .. units .. " / hour")
end
```

We can access, and even change, any variable located in the velocity table by using a LuaRef object. The following code sample demonstrates this:

```
LuaRef v = getGlobal(L, "velocity");
v["y"] = 6
v["units"] = "km"

v["debug"]();
```

Summary

In this chapter, we covered how to use a Lua binding library, Lua Bridge. Lua Bridge fits into a C++ workflow better than the Lua C API does. Because of its clever use of templates, Lua Bridge is far less verbose than the equivalent Lua C API code. Doing more in a smaller amount of space is always productive!

In the next chapter, we will take a look at where to go from here, covering more Lua resources and some tips on where to apply your Lua knowledge.

8
Next Steps

This last chapter is going to focus on looking ahead at where to go next. By now, you should have a fairly strong grasp of the Lua language and some of its more advanced features. But how can you apply all this knowledge and, just as importantly, where can you go to learn more? These are the questions this chapter focuses on. This chapter will include information on the following:

- Books written about Lua
- Game engines powered by Lua
- Games that can be modified with Lua
- Software that can be scripted using Lua

Books

There are many books written about Lua. Some focus on using the language as a standalone tool, others on how to use the language in an embedded scripting environment. Here is a list of additional book resources in no particular order.

Programming In Lua

Ierusalimschy, Roberto. *Programming in Lua, 4th edition*. Lua.Org, 2016.

ISBN13: 9788590379867

Programming in Lua (PIL) is written by the creators of Lua. The book takes an example-based approach to teaching—many of the non trivial concepts in the book are explained with real world code samples. The *first* edition of *Programming in Lua* is available online, for free.

Learning Game AI Programming with Lua

Young, David. *Learning Game AI Programming with Lua: Leverage the Power of Lua Programming to Create Game AI That Focuses on Motion, Animation, and Tactics.* Packt Publishing, 2014.

ISBN 13: 9781783281336

This book focuses on learning to program game AI in a Lua sandbox environment. The sandbox is a great example of how to build a 3D game framework in C++ and embed Lua as a scripting language. By using Lua, this book avoids requiring low-level engine code and allows the reader to focus on AI.

LÖVE for Lua Game Programming

Akinlaja, Damilare Darmie. *LOVE For Lua Game Programming.* Packt Publishing, 2013.

ISBN 13: 9781782161608

This book follows a tutorial approach with examples and step-by-step instructions to help explain the key concepts of the LÖVE framework as well as everything you need to know about game development using the Lua programming language. The book is a great introduction to the LÖVE framework for anyone interested in game development.

Lua Game Development Cookbook

Kašuba Mário. *Lua Game Development Cookbook.* Packt Publishing, 2015.

ISBN 13: 9781849515504

The Lua Game Development Cookbook contains over 70 recipes for creating games using Lua. The book covers a wide array of topics such as 2D game development, 3D game development, UI development, game physics, audio, and AI. By the end of the book, you will have all the knowledge required to make complete games using Lua.

Game Development with Lua

Schuytema, P. and Manyen, M. *Game Development with Lua*. Charles River Media, 2005.

ISBN 13: 9781584504047

Game Development with Lua focuses on how to use Lua as a game scripting language effectively. The book focuses heavily on embedding Lua into a C/C++ game engine, with the goal of being able to rapidly prototype games. Some common use cases, such as using Lua to build GUI systems, event handling, and AI state machines, are also covered.

Beginning Lua Programming

Jung, K. and Brown, A. *Beginning Lua Programming*. Wrox Press, 2007.

ISBN 13: 978-0470069172

Aimed at those new to programming, *Beginning Lua Programming* assumes no prior programming knowledge. The book focuses on teaching Lua trough lengthy, practical examples with a conversational tone. Both the Lua language and the Lua C API are covered. One of the more unique topics the book covers is how to use Lua for modifying and serving HTML pages.

Lua Programming Gems

Figueiredo, L. H.; Celes, W.; Ierusalimschy, R., eds. *Lua Programming Gems*. Lua.org, 2008.

ISBN 13: 9788590379843

Lua Programming Gems is a collection of articles that capture some Lua best practices as well as clever solutions to difficult problems. The book contains gems related to both game and non-game contexts. Algorithms, data structures, and design patterns are all covered in an easy to follow, comprehensive style.

Learn Lua for iOS Game Development

Varma, Jayant. *Learn Lua for iOS Game Development*. Apress, 2012.

ISBN 13: 9781430246626

Learn Lua for iOS Game Development aims to introduce Lua as an alternative for Objective C. The book has a very detailed section on the Gideros framework, which streamlines many common tasks for game development like scene management and loading textures. The book also has a very detailed section on the math essential to making games.

Game engines

Because of its embeddable nature and lightweight runtime, Lua is a great fit for game technology. Many game engines and frameworks use Lua as an embedded scripting language, making game development quick and easy. Here is a list of game engines that offer support for Lua as an embedded scripting language.

LÖVE 2D

LÖVE 2D is a free, open source game framework available at `https://love2d.org`.

Love is a very powerful 2D framework for making games with Lua. It is built on top of SDL, making both cross-platform support and gamepad support very reliable. Love is a very small and easy to use framework, it's well suited for both beginners and professionals alike. Love has a Wiki, which serves as a getting started guide—it is online at `https://love2d.org/wiki/Main_Page`.

Defold

Defold is a free lightweight 2D game engine from King, available at `https://www.defold.com`.

Defold provides you with everything you need to make a game. It has a full-featured editor which offers tools for creating UI, animation, authoring physics, designing levels, and much more. The engine offers fast, live iteration through code hot reloading. Hot reloading code means whenever you make a code change, it can be hot loaded without having to restart the game. Defold offers a large number of tutorials for learning the engine; these tutorials are online at `https://www.defold.com/tutorials/getting-started/`.

Corona

Corona is a free game engine available at `https://coronalabs.com`.

Corona offers very fast iteration times with a live rebuild option. This means you can build and deploy an application once, and see changes happen live on a device as you are making them. Corona is unique because it is not only a game engine, but also a publishing and user acquisition service. There are several books for getting started with Corona, like *Corona SDK Hotshot*, by Flanagan, Nevin or *Corona SDK Mobile Game Development: Beginner's Guide* by Fernandez, Michelle; both books are published by Packt Publishing.

Leadwerks

Leadwerks is an easy-to-use 3D game engine available at `https://www.leadwerks.com`.

Learwerks focuses on ease of use and ease of learning. It is a very approachable 3D game engine for those just starting out making games. Leadwerks provides a marketplace for purchasing both 3D and 2D assets. There is a very active community on the Leadwerks forums at `https://www.leadwerks.com/community/`.

Gideros

Gideros is a free, open source game framework available at `http://giderosmobile.com`.

Gideros comes with all the tools you need to deploy a game, such as a lightweight IDE, players for desktop and mobile devices, a texture packer, and a font creator; there are also third-party tools. Gideros uses an object-oriented approach to game creation—it provides a simple Lua class system. The core framework can be extended using plugins, which are written in native code such as C++, Java, or Objective C. You can try Gideros live and online at `http://giderosmobile.com/code/`.

Urho 3D

Urho 3D is a free, open source game engine available at `https://urho3d.github.io`.

Urho is written in C++, with bindings to Lua and LuaJIT. The Lua API provided by Urho exposes almost everything that the C++ API does. The engine is written with a focus on 3D games, but 2D games can easily be developed using Urho as well. A good way to learn Urho 3D's Lua API is by browsing the official samples at `https://github.com/urho3d/Urho3D/tree/master/bin/Data/LuaScripts`.

Polycode

Polycode is a free, open source framework for making games and interactive applications. It is available from `http://polycode.org`.

Polycode is well suited to making both 2D and 3D games as well as non-game applications. The framework provides an IDE for both world editing and writing Lua code. Polycode runs on all major platforms. The Polycode website has a section for learning how to use the framework at `http://polycode.org/learn/`.

ShiVa

ShiVa is a commercial 3D game engine available at `https://www.shiva-engine.com`.

ShiVa provides all of the features one would expect from a modern 3D game engine such as resource management, scene management, physics, UI, a terrain system, and more. It is a cross-platform game engine, with the editor being available on macOS, Windows, and Linux. To learn more about using the engine, check out *Learning ShiVa3D Game Development* by Wade Tracy, published by Packt publishing.

Game mods

Lua's highly flexible and easy-to-embed nature makes it appealing not only for game engines, but games as well. Several games provide a very large, comprehensive Lua API with the intention of allowing hobbyists to modify and extend the base game. Often these mods lack official documentation, but they tend to have a large active community to make up for it.

Roblox

Roblox is not exactly a game; it's a platform for building games. However, Roblox resembles a game more than an engine, which is why it's listed as a game. Roblox allows users to create and share games using Roblox Studio. It exposes programming through Lua, which exposes an object-oriented Lua API.

You can get started with Roblox development at `http://robloxdev.com/learn-roblox/coding-scripts`.

Garry's Mod

Garry's Mod is a physics sandbox game which started out as a mod for Half Life 2. In the version 9 release, Lua scripting was added. Players can script weapons, vehicles, entities, NPCs, and much more using Lua. Scripted mods even work in multiplayer sessions.

To get started with the Garry's Mod Lua API, check out the official tutorials available online at `https://wiki.garrysmod.com/page/Beginner_Tutorial_Intro`.

World Of Warcraft

World of Warcraft (**WOW**) is a massively multiplayer online role playing game developed by Blizzard Entertainment. WOW exposes a subset of Lua 5.1, allowing players to customize the game interface.

The recommended book about writing Lua interfaces for WOW is *Beginning Lua with World of Warcraft Add-ons* by Paul Emmerich, published by Apress.

Natural Selection 2

Natural Selection 2 is a mix between a first-person shooter and a real-time strategy game developed by Unknown Worlds Entertainment. The game was designed to be very easy to mod. Lua is not only used as an extension to mod the game, but much of the official game is written in Lua as well. This lets players go in and modify the base game very easily.

Learn more about modding for Natural Selection 2 at the Unknown Worlds Wiki at `https://wiki.unknownworlds.com/ns2/Modding`.

Don't Starve

Don't Starve is a survival sandbox game developed by Klei Entertainment. Much of the game is written in Lua, which makes the game easy to mod. User can create custom items, characters, scenarios, world objects and more using Lua 5.1. Don't Starve and its multiplayer version Don't Starve Together both have a very large and active modding community.

To get started with modding Don't Starve, check out the modding section on Klei's forum at `https://forums.kleientertainment.com/files/category/5-modding-tools-tutorials-examples/`.

Hack 'n' Slash

Hack 'n' Slash, developed by Double Fine Productions, uses Lua scripting as a core game mechanic. This mechanic makes the gameplay rather open ended, while the game itself does have an end goal. Hack 'n' Slash is built on top of the Moai SDK—all of the game's Lua code can be edited.

Get the game at `https://store.steampowered.com/app/246070/Hack_n_Slash/`.

Scriptable software

Lua is particularly well suited to be used as an embedded scripting language. Many existing software packages leverage Lua to provide users with the ability to the base of the software. All of the software listed below can be extended using Lua.

CEGUI

Crazy Eddie's GUI (CEGUI) is a user interface system written in C++, often used for video games. CEGUI offers a Lua backend scripting module, which allows user interfaces to be built using Lua. The CEGUI library is easy to embed, and the Lua API it exposes allows for Lua to issue callbacks to the application that is embedding it.

The website is `http://cegui.org.uk`.

Conky

Conky is a desktop system monitor written for the X Window System. Conky is available on Linux, Free BSD, and Open BSD. Conky can be extended with Lua to offer and display information that is otherwise not available to the base software.

The website is `https://github.com/brndnmtthws/conky`.

Premake

Premake is used to generate build files for IDEs such as Visual Studio, X Code, Mono Develop, Code::Blocks, and more. Premake makes managing cross-platform projects easier by removing the need to manually update build files for every platform's IDE; instead it generates these files for you. Premake files that define how a project should be structured are just Lua files.

The website is `https://premake.github.io`.

Moho

Moho is vector-based 2D animation software developed by Smith Micro Software. Most of the tools Moho offers are all scripted in Lua. Users can extend the software and create custom tools using Lua. Documentation for the Moho Lua API is online at `http://mohoscripting.com`.

The website is `https://my.smithmicro.com/anime-studio-debut.html`.

Summary

 This book tried to cover everything you need to program in Lua. We started with setting up Lua and the tools needed to run it. Next, we covered all of the information needed to program in Lua, from basic concepts such as loops to advanced concepts such as object oriented programming. Embedding Lua as a scripting language and using Lua Bridge to reduce the amount of code needed to embed Lua was also discussed. Finally, this last chapter provided some guidance on where to go next to learn more about Lua and some applications that can be used with your Lua knowledge.

Other Books You May Enjoy

If you enjoyed this book, you may be interested in these other books by Packt:

Embedded Systems Architecture
Daniele Lacamera

ISBN: 978-1-78883-250-2

- Participate in the design and definition phase of an embedded product
- Get to grips with writing code for ARM Cortex-M microcontrollers
- Build an embedded development lab and optimize the workflow
- Write memory-safe code
- Understand the architecture behind the communication interfaces
- Understand the design and development patterns for connected and distributed devices in the IoT
- Master multitask parallel execution patterns and real-time operating systems

Embedded Linux Development Using Yocto Project Cookbook - Second Edition
Alex González

ISBN: 978-1-78839-921-0

- Optimize your Yocto Project setup to speed up development and debug build issues
- Use Docker containers to build Yocto Project-based systems
- Take advantage of the user-friendly Toaster web interface to the Yocto Project build system
- Build and debug the Linux kernel and its device trees
- Customize your root filesystem with already-supported and new Yocto packages
- Optimize your production systems by reducing the size of both the Linux kernel and root filesystems
- Explore the mechanisms to increase the root filesystem security
- Understand the open source licensing requirements and how to comply with them when cohabiting with proprietary programs
- Create recipes, and build and run applications in C, C++, Python, Node.js, and Java

Leave a review - let other readers know what you think

Please share your thoughts on this book with others by leaving a review on the site that you bought it from. If you purchased the book from Amazon, please leave us an honest review on this book's Amazon page. This is vital so that other potential readers can see and use your unbiased opinion to make purchasing decisions, we can understand what our customers think about our products, and our authors can see your feedback on the title that they have worked with Packt to create. It will only take a few minutes of your time, but is valuable to other potential customers, our authors, and Packt. Thank you!

Index